"A model of evangelistic preaching! Highly recommended!"

– Michael Eaton, Chrisco Central Church, Nairobi, Kenya

"The message of Isaiah 53 is unpacked with a new freshness, and sets forth the glory of Jesus Christ in His humiliation and His exaltation. His salvation is presented in compelling terms and the reader is continually challenged to a personal response throughout."

– S. John Dixon, Minister-Emeritus, 1st Antrim Presbyterian Church, and Former Moderator of the Presbyterian Church of Ireland

"This is the most important question to ask, and here is the most insightful and inspirational answer I have ever read."

– Canon J.John

"RT is blessed with a distinctive, almost unique, skill to take Scripture in all its majesty and interpret it to us right where we live. Now he turns his attention to the sublime Isaiah 53. You will be stirred, edified and strengthened by his insights, love for truth and ability to feed your soul."

– Terry Virgo, Newfrontiers

"RT writes as he is. The man always comes through in his message, which is full of careful, logical, investigative exploration of the text and all that lies around it. His love of the land of Israel only serves to amplify his love of scripture. The combination is powerful – eye-opening, and at times positively breath-taking.

"This is a book to stir your heart, engage your brain and bring to you ever more clearly the wonder of this Jesus - the person to whom RT has surrendered his life, and devoted his years.

"Seat belts will need to be adjusted for this ride. It's a rollercoaster excursion into the heart of God and the love He expressed in Jesus."

"RT has done it again! In an age when the true nature of the Gospel is being seriously questioned, RT takes us back to biblical basics. This is a masterly and deeply inspiring exposition."

WHY JESUS DIED

A Meditation on Isaiah 53

R. T. Kendall

MONARCH
BOOKS
Oxford, UK & Grand Rapids, Michigan, USA

First published in the UK in 2011 by Monarch Books
(a publishing imprint of Lion Hudson plc)
Wilkinson House, Jordan Hill Road, Oxford OX2 8DR, England
Tel: +44 (0)1865 302750 Fax: +44 (0)1865 302757
Email: monarch@lionhudson.com
www.lionhudson.com

Reprinted 2012.

ISBN 978 0 85721 061 6 (print)
ISBN 978 0 85721 220 7 (epub)
ISBN 978 0 85721 219 1 (Kindle)
ISBN 978 0 85721 221 4 (PDF)

Distributed by:
UK: Marston Book Services, PO Box 269, Abingdon, Oxon, OX14 4YN
USA: Kregel Publications, PO Box 2607, Grand Rapids, Michigan 49501

British Library Cataloguing Data

A catalogue record for this book is available from the British Library.

Printed and bound in the UK by Clays Ltd, St Ives plc.

IN MEMORY OF CHARLIE STRIDE (1929–2006)

Preface

This book is an edited version of my twelve sermons on Isaiah 53. I first preached them at Westminster Chapel between January and March in 1986. When people ask me how I manage to write so many books, my answer partly is that a good number of them are based on sermons I have preached in Westminster Chapel, London. In my twenty-five years there I preached approximately three and a half thousand times! Many of these sermons remain unpublished. Only God knows if they will be useful in the future. Tony Collins, publisher of Monarch Books, asked to print these sermons on Isaiah 53, and he suggested the title: *Why Jesus Died.*

I thank Beryl Grogan, my former secretary at the Chapel, for carefully and painstakingly typing every word of the original sermons from a tape recorder. From these, I was able to produce the book you hold in your hands. My successor, Greg Haslam, has graciously allowed Beryl to do a few things for me since our retirement in February 2002.

This is my first book with Monarch. It has been a pleasure to reunite with Tony Collins. When Tony was an editor with Hodder & Stoughton several years ago – during our early days at the Chapel – he helped with a number of my books. I wish to thank yet another former Hodder editor, David Moloney, who has kindly done the final editing of the present book.

I am dedicating *Why Jesus Died* to the memory of Charlie Stride, the London taxi driver who became one of our most popular and faithful members in Westminster Chapel. Of the countless people who professed faith in Christ from the efforts of our Pilot Lights ministry – witnessing in the streets between Buckingham Palace and Victoria – Charlie's conversion was one of the most memorable. He became not only a member of the Chapel but was one of our most involved – with the young and old and everybody in between. Everybody loved Charlie. He went to Heaven since our retirement and I look forward to meeting him there one day.

May God use this book to draw many to Christ, and I pray it will be a blessing to you.

R. T. Kendall
Hendersonville, Tennessee
May 2011

Contents

Foreword

In an informal survey, one hundred Jews on the streets of Tel Aviv were asked: "Who do you think the fifty-third chapter of Isaiah describes?" Most were unfamiliar with the passage and were asked to read it before answering. After doing so, many conceded that they did not know to whom it referred, but some thought it sounded a lot like Jesus.

In my estimation, when it comes to making the case for Jesus, Isaiah 53 is the one chapter in the Hebrew Scriptures that stands above all others. And when it comes to excellent expositors of the word of God, I can't think of but a handful that could unpack it with such skill and biblical insight as Dr R. T. Kendall. What a great pairing!

I was not disappointed. As I read through these twelve chapters of *Why Jesus Died* I discovered a treasure trove of biblical gems and practical applications for both the student of the Bible as well as the seeker.

Actually, I wish this book had been around when I, as a Jew, was on my journey to faith in Jesus many years ago. I would have resonated with the clear-thinking presentation style and the wonderful illustrations that make this passage so relevant today. While Dr Kendall is quick to point out that the seeker of God's truth needs the illumination of the Holy Spirit to see Jesus as the "pierced one" of Isaiah 53:6, the evidence he presents is powerful. The suffering servant of Isaiah's Gospel is indeed the Jesus who died at Calvary. If you have not come to that conclusion, I encourage you to read on with a heart open and ready to hear from God.

Susan Perlman

Associate Executive Director

Jews for Jesus

CHAPTER ONE

Why Would Anyone Believe in Jesus?

*Who has believed our message and to whom
has the arm of the Lord been revealed?*

ISAIAH 53:1

Isaiah 53 is arguably the greatest chapter in the Bible. Charles Spurgeon (1834–92) called it "the Bible in miniature, the Gospel at its essence". It is the leading messianic text of the Old Testament and is referred to by the early church more than any other passage. It points to the person and mission of Jesus – his life, death, resurrection, ascension, and intercession – more than any other Old Testament passage. It also lays the theological foundation for the Gospel like no other. It points both to the crucifixion and the atonement of Christ in a manner that sounds as though Isaiah 53 were written as history rather than prophecy. Indeed, it is as if Isaiah was an eye witness to what was going on between Good Friday and Easter – and even to Christ's intercession!

And yet Isaiah 53 *is* prophecy – proclaiming with infallible accuracy seven hundred years in advance what Jesus would be like and what he would do. One of the greatest proofs of the divine inspiration of the Bible is *prophecy*. How could anybody know the future? Nobody knows the future. The devil does not know the future. Angels do not know the future. You and I do not know the future. But God knows the future – perfectly. And when, by the Holy Spirit, he gives information about the future to his chosen servants and it is written down, you can count on the reliability of that word. "Above all, you must understand," said Peter, "that no prophecy of Scripture came about by the prophet's own interpretation. For prophecy never had its origin in the will of man, but men spoke from God as they were carried along by the Holy Spirit" (2 Peter 1:20– 21). Indeed, said Paul, "All Scripture is God-breathed and is useful for teaching, rebuking, correcting and training in righteousness, so that the man of God may be thoroughly equipped for every good work" (2 Timothy 3:16–17).

An angel of the Lord said to Philip: "Go south to the road – the desert road – that goes down from Jerusalem to Gaza" (Acts 8:26). Philip had no idea why he would be given directions like that, but he went. He came to a chariot where a man happened to be reading from Isaiah 53. The Holy Spirit told Philip to go to the chariot, and Philip asked the man in the chariot (an Ethiopian eunuch) if he understood what he was reading. The man replied: "How can I unless someone explains it to me?" Philip accepted an invitation to sit in the chariot to explain these words:

He was led like a sheep to the slaughter, and as a lamb before the shearer is silent, so he did not open his mouth. In his humiliation he was deprived of justice. Who can speak of his descendants? For his life was taken from the earth.

(ACTS 8:32–33; CF. ISAIAH 53:7–8)

Then Philip, beginning with that very passage of Scripture, told the Ethiopian "the good news about Jesus" (Acts 8:35). I love the King James translation: Philip "preached unto him *Jesus*". That verse represents the tip of the iceberg of how the early church felt about Isaiah 53. It was *all about Jesus*.

Most modern Jewish writers (sadly) refuse to see the Messiah in this passage, although their predecessors for some reason weren't so biased. Many ancient rabbis understood Isaiah as referring to the promised Messiah. For example, the first-century rabbi Jonathan ben Uziel paraphrased his Targum (the Aramaic translation of the Hebrew Old Testament) to read: "My servant, the Messiah, will be great, who was bruised for our sins" (verse 5). That is the way the early church interpreted this passage. And yet the truth is that all attempts to explain Isaiah 53 as anything other than reference to the Messiah are palpable failures.

The name Jesus does not appear in Isaiah 53, but its

recurring themes – vicarious suffering, total obedience, utter willingness to suffer, the guilt of the people of God, the Lord laying on him our iniquity, being cut off from the land of the living, being numbered with the transgressors, the divine approval – all point to Jesus of Nazareth and what he did by dying on the cross. Prophecy rarely refers to a person's actual name in advance (as in 1 Kings 13:2 and Isaiah 45:1) but normally portrays the person or situation in a way that, once they have come to pass, leaves no doubt to the *believer*. This is a key: it is for the believer. Faith is a prerequisite in grasping prophecy in advance as well as seeing it clearly in its fulfillment. God never instructs his prophets to forecast the future in a way that removes the need for faith. Neither is the fulfillment of prophecy so definite that faith is no longer required. The exception to the latter would be the Second Coming of Jesus: "Look, he is coming with the clouds, and every eye will see him, even those who pierced him; and all the peoples of the earth will mourn because of him. So shall it be! Amen" (Revelation 1:7). There will be no doubting then! But all fulfilled prophecies in advance of the Last Day will require faith – which is partly why the Jews missed their Messiah. They needed a "sign" and no sign was given; only the prophet's word (Matthew 12:39; cf. 1 Corinthians 1:22).

When I was the minister of Westminster Chapel in London we started a street ministry on Saturdays – called Pilot Lights – giving out Gospel tracts and talking about Jesus to passers-by in the streets of Victoria and Westminster. I did this in Buckingham Gate for the last twenty years of my ministry there. It so happened that, on the Saturday before I began my original sermons on Isaiah 53, we witnessed the most memorable conversion from our Pilot Light ministry. Charlie Stride, a London taxi driver, had been given my tract "What is Christianity?" by a member of the scheme the week before. He read it the same day and was "shaken rigid", he said. Charlie drove to the Chapel the following Saturday to find answers to the questions he had about the pamphlet. He said he had read it again several times over the previous week. He asked me: "Are you the one who wrote this tract?" "Yes." "I've never been so shaken in my whole life," he said to me. He invited me to sit with him in the back seat of his taxi (which I was very pleased to do on that cold January day). "I've had a thousand people in the last thirty years giving me tracts like this. I don't know why I didn't tear this one up as I did the others. But it made me see I am afraid to die. I never thought I would believe in Hell until now." It was a classic case of the convicting power of the Holy Spirit.

Two questions were on Charlie's mind. His first question was about Jews: "Will Jews go to Hell if they don't receive Jesus?" He asked this because many of his fellow taxi drivers were Jews. I replied: "I'm afraid that is true." The other question was: "According to this tract, if I don't do what it says for me to do then I am going to Hell – is that right?" I replied: "I'm afraid it is." Instead of being offended (as people often are regarding such matters), he was in tears. Like a ripe fruit waiting to be plucked, he was yearning to know what to do next. I presented the same Gospel to him as will be unfolded in this book. He received it with his whole heart. It was a thrilling day for him of course, but I have to say it was also one of the sweetest moments of my twenty-five years in London. I later baptized Charlie; he became a member of the Chapel and was one of the most beloved people ever to pass our way. On the night of my farewell to the Chapel in 2002 he gave his testimony. Since our retirement he has gone to Heaven.

Isaiah's opening word in this chapter raises the question: why believe in Jesus? "Who has believed our message?" You may want to ask: "Why would a *Jew* believe in Jesus?" But I ask: "Why would *anyone* believe in Jesus?" Indeed, why should they? There are actually two questions that open Isaiah 53:1) "Who has believed our message?"; and 2) "To whom is the arm of the Lord revealed?" That latter question implies that one needs a *revelation* in order for a person to believe the message.

A frequent question people often ask after their conversion is: "Why did I not see this before?" One of the most memorable converts from my old Lauderdale Manors Baptist Church in Fort Lauderdale, Florida, was a man named George Bellamy. He was fifty when he was saved. After a church service sometime later I saw him looking at the sky with tears running down his face. I said: "Is there anything wrong, George?" "No," he assured me. "I am only asking why I took so long to see all this." I looked at him and said: "But, George, some people sadly *never* see what you have come to see. Instead of regretting the wasted years just be thankful that you have come to see this even at your age!"

The faith that saves is a gift of God. "For it is by grace you have been saved, through faith – and this not from yourselves, it is the gift of God" (Ephesians 2:8). One can believe only by the enabling and sovereign grace of the Holy Spirit. "The Spirit gives life" (John 6:63). God said to Moses: "'I will have mercy on whom I have mercy, and I will have compassion on whom I will have compassion.' It does not, therefore, depend on man's desire or effort, but on God's mercy" (Romans 9:15–16; cf. Exodus 33:19). When a person believes, it is not a person "working up faith", because of the sheer mercy and compassion of God. There is nothing sufficiently good in any of us that would force God to show his mercy. But if he is pleased to show it, we can only thank him. We will never be able to thank him enough.

Why then does *anybody* believe? Answer: it is owing to the mercy of God. Not only that; when a person is given faith they are immediately ready to obey – and ask: "What next?" The Ethiopian eunuch believed and even asked to be baptized (Acts 8:36).

We may ask the question: "Why doesn't everybody see this truth about Jesus?" But another question is: "Why does *anybody* see it?"

The context of Isaiah 53

Isaiah had been describing Jesus in the closing verses of Isaiah 52, the immediate context for Isaiah 53:

> See, my servant will act wisely; he will be raised
> and lifted up and highly exalted. Just as there were
> many who were appalled at him – his appearance
> was so disfigured beyond that of any man and his
> form marred beyond human likeness – so will he
> sprinkle many nations, and kings will shut their
> mouths because of him. For what they were not told,
> they will see, and what they have not heard, they will
> understand.
>
> (ISAIAH 52:13–15)

This indicates not only the wisdom of Jesus – he "will act wisely" – but also his exaltation following his horrific crucifixion. Many would be "appalled", said Isaiah. If you saw Mel Gibson's film about the crucifixion of Jesus you were possibly shocked, horrified, and in disbelief. But it is very likely that what Jesus endured was even worse than what was portrayed in that film. According to Isaiah his appearance was "disfigured beyond that of any man and his form marred beyond human likeness". It was enough to put anybody off. He was almost unrecognizable. The disciples forsook him and fled (Matthew 26:56). His mother Mary and Mary Magdalene stayed through the ordeal however.

But something else happened as a consequence of that crucifixion. The Messiah would "sprinkle many nations" – a reference to the sprinkling of his blood upon the many peoples of the earth. Isaiah saw this in advance: that the Messiah would suffer, die, be resurrected and exalted – and sprinkle his blood upon many. Not only that; kings would "shut their mouths because of him". Every mouth would be "silenced", said Paul (Romans 3:19; "stopped" in the KJV), but according to Isaiah even kings would be silenced. It means there would be nothing they could say. There is more: "that which has not been told them they will see" (Isaiah 52:15, ESV); that is, they will see things clearly eventually. Kings would be astonished at the unexpected happening within their nations. This also shows that all people will bow the knee to God's Messiah one day. And that which they have not heard, "they will understand". The question is: when? When would they understand? Would it be when it is too late – and "every eye sees" at Jesus' Second Coming? Or could it be that in God's mercy the Lord will lift their blindness by letting them *hear* – and heal their deafness in advance of that final day?

It is in this context, then, that Isaiah raises these two questions: "Who has believed our message and to whom has the arm of the Lord been revealed?"

The name Jesus – the only name that makes sense of Isaiah 53 – was withheld from Israel generally for hundreds of years. It was first revealed to Joseph, the adopted father of Jesus. What an honour given to him by God: "Joseph, son of David, do not be afraid to take Mary home as your wife, because what is conceived in her is from the Holy Spirit. She will give birth to a son, and *you are to give him the name Jesus*, because he will save his people from their sins" (Matthew 1:20–21).

Isaiah 53 was written in such a way that those who do accept this message by faith inwardly know they have got it right. It is an earmark of true faith that you are assured and know you have not been deceived. As to the two questions, "Who has believed our message?" and "To whom has the arm of the Lord been revealed?", the answer is: "Those whom God is seeking." They are the ones who believed Isaiah's message and the ones to whom the arm of the Lord has been revealed. As a consequence of God seeking them, they are inwardly persuaded. This is also called the inner testimony of the Holy Spirit.

If God is on one's case, one is also known by different identities in the Bible: "his people" (Matthew 1:21), "his own" (John 1:11), "the church of God" (Acts 20:28), "the elect" (Matthew 24:24), "his own sheep" (John 10:3), "whom God has chosen" (Romans 8:33), "objects of his mercy" (Romans 9:23), "loved by God and called" (Romans 1:7). Jesus even said to certain Jews: "You do not believe because you are not my sheep" (John 10:26). But if you are one of his sheep – whether Jew or Gentile – you know his voice. "My sheep hear my voice," said Jesus (John 10:27, ESV).

The picture we also see in Isaiah is that of the prophet writing in language that, strange as it may seem, is designed to keep people from believing. This may give you pause but there are times when God keeps people from believing. The same Isaiah was told, after his vision of the glory of God:

> Go and tell this people: "Be ever hearing, but never understanding; be ever seeing, but never perceiving." Make the heart of this people calloused; make their ears dull and close their eyes. Otherwise they might see with their eyes, hear with their ears, understand with their hearts, and turn and be healed.
>
> (ISAIAH 6:9–10)

Jesus applied this word in Isaiah to his own parables (Matthew 13:14–15). He also said that the devil may step in where the Word was sown, and "takes away the word from their hearts, *so that they may not believe and be saved*" (Luke 8:12). Do I understand this? No. But for some reason God uses the devil as his tool to keep people from seeing the truth. Like it or not – and I don't say I like it – God is not going to save everybody.

To put it another way, the context of this passage – Isaiah 52:14 ("his appearance was so disfigured beyond that of any man") refers to the offer of the Gospel to all people but in such a way that puts everybody off! This means that if this Gospel does not offend you or me there is hope for us! There was nothing attractive about the crucifixion of Jesus. Nothing. And yet Paul determined "to know nothing while I was with you except Jesus Christ and him *crucified*"

(1 Corinthians 2:2). The very thing that – at the natural level – is designed to put people off is what Paul was preoccupied with when he came to Corinth. He reckoned that if anybody could accept something so offensive it would only be because God was sovereignly at work. Those who would be *unashamed* of the cross would be those that are variously called "his own", "his people", "his sheep", and so on.

Are you ashamed of the cross?

One of the first things you discover after your conversion is that God has been on your case for a long time. You can look back and see his glorious hand, his providence, his protection and guidance. So when God finds us we become aware that he is in control of everything and always has been! You realize that God is in control. You become aware that he was always aware of you. You once thought he didn't care; you now see that he cares more about you than you do yourself! You realize that God has known you from the foundation of the world.

> He called me long before I heard, before my sinful
> heart was stirred;
> But when I took Him at His word, forgiven He
> lifted me.
> From sinking sand He lifted me, with tender hand
> He lifted me,
> From shades of night to plains of light, O praise his
> name, He lifted me!

CHARLES H. GABRIEL (1856–1932)

And yet there is a paradox – if you can accept it: although not all will be saved, God has nonetheless made a provision for everybody. Jesus died for everybody who ever lived. The only way I can be absolutely certain that Jesus died for me is the knowledge that he died for everybody. This includes you. He died for you on the cross. If you want to be saved, transfer the trust you have had in your good works to what Jesus did for you on the cross. As long as you are trusting your good works, you are showing contempt (even if you didn't mean to) for why Jesus died. When you are truly broken – as Charlie Stride was – you will yearn for this Gospel. In a word: the good news is that you are saved by trusting Jesus Christ and his blood – not by your good works. Here is what Paul said:

> For since in the wisdom of God the world through its wisdom did not know him, God was pleased through the foolishness of what was preached to save those who believe. Jews demand miraculous signs and Greeks look for wisdom, but we preach Christ crucified: a stumbling-block to Jews and foolishness to Gentiles, but to those whom God has called, both Jews and Greeks, Christ the power of God and the wisdom of God.
>
> (1 CORINTHIANS 1:21-24)

God's Messiah – also called God's Son (Isaiah 9:6) – was not revealed after all as a great political, economic, social or military leader (which Jews anticipated), but rather as the Lamb of God who was to die on a cross for our sins.

Have you ever noticed – or wondered why – Jesus did not try to get people to believe in him? Jesus had the power, if he chose to use it, to save every person he met. But he was not trying to add numbers to his following. Indeed, "the Son gives life to whom he is pleased to give it" (John 5:21). He was not going around trying to make converts. He knew that those very people the Father gave him would come to him (John 6:37). "My sheep hear my voice, and I know them, and they follow me" (John 10:27, ESV).

Jesus' own brothers did not even believe in him – at least for a while. They were cynical about him despite knowing of his miracles. "You ought to leave here and go to Judea," they said disingenuously to him, "so that your disciples may see the miracles you do. No one who wants to become a public figure acts in secret. Since you are doing these things, show yourself to the world" (John 7:3–4). Despite Jesus' miracles, they "did not believe in him" (John 7:5). Miracles do not convince if the Holy Spirit does not do the convincing. Even if you see them! You will still find something to justify unbelief! Some people even personally witnessed Jesus raising Lazarus from the dead but maintained a sceptical, cynical perspective. While some eye-witnesses were thrilled and amazed, others queried: "Could not he who opened the eyes of the blind man have kept this man from dying?" (John 11:37). This goes to show that miracles do not necessarily cause people to have faith.

Some sceptics often say they would believe in God – or in Jesus – if they saw a miracle. But this is not necessarily the case. God can – and sometimes does – use the miraculous to get one's attention (see John 4:29–30). But if the Holy Spirit is not present to create faith, any person – even in the face of a thousand miracles – will remain unconvinced, unconverted and in unbelief.

What makes faith *faith*?

Behind the entire account of Lazarus' being raised from the dead in John 11 is the answer to the oldest philosophical question in the world: why does an omnipotent and kind God allow evil and suffering? The answer is: in order that people might have faith. Does this surprise you? You perhaps thought that God's allowing evil was the very thing that lets them doubt his existence. I know what you mean. But there is another way to see it. For example, when Mary and Martha sent word to Jesus that their brother Lazarus was sick they assumed he would go immediately to Bethany in order to heal Lazarus and therefore keep him from dying. But he didn't. He stayed put. This made no sense to anyone at the time. They all knew that it was within Jesus' own power to keep Lazarus from dying. Surely a loving God with all power would heal him! But Jesus remained where he was and allowed Lazarus to die. His immediate explanation to his mystified disciples was: "I am glad I was not there [in Bethany where Lazarus was], *so that you may believe*"

(John 11:15). In other words, he needed to train his disciples – including Martha and Mary – what faith was and what makes faith, faith. In a nutshell: if one "believes" because he has the evidence, such "believing" does not warrant the title *faith*. What makes faith *faith* is that you believe without evidence – only trusting God who has spoken by his word. "Faith is being sure of what we hope for and certain of what *we do not see*" (Hebrews 11:1; "assurance of things hoped for, the conviction of things not seen", in the ESV).

To give another example, the Jews who mocked Jesus at his crucifixion said: "Come down now from the cross, that we may *see and believe*" (Mark 15:32). Note the order: first "see", then "believe". But this is not faith. When you "see" first, followed by "believing", such "believing" it is no longer true faith. Faith is to believe *without the tangible evidence*.

So why does God allow suffering? Answer: to make room for faith. If you and I had the answer to this immortal question, "Why does God allow evil?", we would never – ever – need faith! What makes faith a possibility is that you *don't* know the answer to this ancient question. *Be glad that you don't know* why God allows evil and suffering so that you qualify for faith. For example, when "every eye" shall see Jesus in his glory at the Second Coming, they will "believe" – oh yes, will they ever! But it won't be faith at work; it will be sight.

Jesus refused Mary and Martha's request because he wanted to teach everybody – his disciples, Mary and Martha, you and me – the nature of true faith. The people there at the time couldn't figure out why the loving Jesus who could have so easily healed Lazarus would let him die. It made no sense at the time. That is, until Jesus showed up four days after Lazarus' funeral and showed them that raising Lazarus from the dead was a better idea than keeping him from dying! You and I therefore can remember this principle: there is a reason God allows suffering. As *nobody* had the remotest idea what Jesus was up to when he did not heal Lazarus, so nobody knows what God is up to when he allows evil and suffering. Mark it down: when God reveals the answer to the question "Why does God allow suffering?", you will see essentially the same kind of scenario unfolding. Letting Lazarus die was a preview of how God will clear his name on that eternal day. No one had any complaints when Jesus raised Lazarus from the dead. And no one will have any complaints when God vindicates his name in the age to come. You and I can go to the stake for this principle.

Let's look at that question: why is it so amazing that *anyone* would believe in Jesus? His appearance was so disfigured beyond that of any man; it was "marred beyond human likeness". It was more than enough to put anybody off. If anybody needed proof that Jesus was no Messiah, the Jews could say: "Look to the cross!" Here is the irony: as believers in the Messiah we point people to the cross. The Jews, convinced he was *not* the Messiah, pointed people to the cross! It was – to them – the ultimate proof that Jesus of Nazareth was getting what he deserved when they crucified him. They believed that no Messiah of God could be crucified; God would not let his Messiah die.

There is an ironic comparison between Muslims and Jews. Muslims do not believe that Jesus was ever crucified because Allah would never allow a true prophet to die on a cross. They believe that Allah delivered Jesus from the cross – that Jesus went straight to Heaven without being crucified. And yet this is a subtle way to avoid seeing Jesus' blood as the remedy for sin. In a rather different way the Jews, too, focused on their "proof" that Jesus was not the Messiah – that God would not allow the promised Messiah to die this hideous death. But this too kept Jews from seeing Jesus' blood as the remedy for sin. Both Muslims and Jews have in common a blindness to the reason Jesus had to die. Satan will always blind men and women from seeing the glory of the substitutionary death of Jesus Christ.

The Jews therefore did not have the slightest problem with their consciences for nailing Jesus' hands to a cross. God would not allow them to proceed had Jesus been the Messiah. The sight of Jesus on the cross was the final straw that laid to rest any claim that this was God's Messiah. As I said above, I doubt if Mel Gibson's film went far enough in demonstrating how awful was his naked, bruised, bloody, swollen and disfigured body. He was forsaken by his followers, left to die alone despite all the miracles people saw. Those who witnessed Lazarus being raised from the dead had disappeared once Jesus was nailed to a cross. They scoffed and said: "Come down now from the cross" (Matthew 27:42).

The question therefore follows: why would *anybody* believe in Jesus?

All that happened on Good Friday two thousand years ago is summed up in a "message" (Isaiah 53:1; or "report" in the AV). What is that message? It is unveiled through "preaching". It pleased God by the "foolishness of what was preached" (or "foolishness of preaching" in the KJV) to save those who believe (1 Corinthians 1:21). No Jew remotely imagined that the long-awaited coming of the Messiah would be made known by such a lowly, unspectacular and undignified method. They felt that the Messiah would be obvious – his very presence would speak for itself!

Isaiah saw this in advance – and asked: "Who will believe it?" He felt the burden in his soul, knowing how this Messiah would come and go and hardly be noticed.

But that was God's idea and plan: namely, that the Messiah would be made known by the foolishness of what was preached. This method need not be limited to a pulpit; anybody can bring this message. But it is imperative that we get it out. "How, then, can they call on the one they have not believed in? And how can they believe in the one of whom they have not heard? And how can they hear without someone preaching to them? And how can they preach unless they are sent?" (Romans 10:14–15). It is done by word of mouth from one person to another. *You* can do it! And when you do you fulfill that ancient word, "How beautiful are the feet of those who bring good news!" (Romans 10:15; cf. Isaiah 52:7).

Moreover, to whom is the "arm of the Lord" revealed? The "arm" was a symbol of soldiers going to battle. The contrast was that women in those days never showed their arms, but a soldier's arm was free and it represented readiness, power and courage in battle. In Isaiah 52:10 the prophet said: "The Lord will lay bare his holy arm in the sight of all the nations." This was only a hint of God's strength and power. And yet God by his little finger could knock us all down in one stroke and we would be flat on the floor. God can raise the dead and heal anybody. He can cure cancer as readily as one could heal a common cold.

God's power was revealed in the weakness of his Messiah. His power was seen in the weakness of the Incarnation. Incarnation means that God became man, the Word was made flesh (John 1:14). The weakness of the Incarnation is seen in the Word ("*logos*" in Greek) inhabiting the womb of the Virgin Mary. It was God becoming vulnerable, and yet, "the foolishness of God is wiser than man's wisdom, and the weakness of God is stronger than man's strength" (1 Corinthians 1:25). Christ was crucified in "weakness" (2 Corinthians 13:4), which showed his immense strength! He could have called ten thousand angels to stop the whole ordeal of wicked men putting him on that cross. He could have struck them dead or blind by his very word. But he chose to appear weak. Only a mighty man could do that.

How then does God show his power? By opening blind eyes and raising the spiritually dead. We are all born blind

(2 Corinthians 4:4) but also spiritually dead (Ephesians 2:1). Only God can heal the blind; only God can raise the dead. It is when the arm of the Lord is laid bare – as when Saul of Tarsus was struck to the ground on the road to Damascus and instantly converted (Acts 9:4ff) – that you know it is something only *he* could do.

To whom, then, is the arm of the Lord revealed? His arm – his power – is revealed to those God is seeking: to those who believe. Could that be you? Believing means to embrace this Messiah as he is revealed in the Bible. You may have to do it completely alone. Your best friend may not go along with you. Your closest relative – a parent or a child – may resent or reject you. It means transferring the trust you have had in your good works to what he has done for you on the cross.

Are you one who has believed this report? Has the arm of the Lord been revealed to you?

CHAPTER TWO

What Did Jesus Look Like?

He grew up before him like a tender shoot,
and like a root out of dry ground. He had
no beauty or majesty to attract us to him,
nothing in his appearance that we should
desire him.

ISAIAH 53:2

The Argentinian evangelist Luis Palau shared this joke with me. A black man and a white man were driving on the interstate and arguing whether Jesus was white or black. "He is white – we all know that!" said the white man. "You are absolutely wrong," said the black man. "Jesus is black!" The argument got so heated that their car crashed and both of them were killed. But on the way up toward the Pearly Gates they continued to argue: "He's white!", "He's black!" Then St Peter said: "Welcome." The two men said: "We want to know whether Jesus is white or black." "Relax, sit down. In a moment you will find out for yourselves," said Peter. In walked Jesus, who greeted them: *"Buenas dias señores!"*

I suppose that joke provides a hint of how many surprises there will be when we get to Heaven. But one thing is certain: we will see Jesus – the same Jesus who died on the cross and ascended to Heaven – and he will look exactly as he did when he was on this earth. He is the same.

A few years ago I had the privilege of preaching to nineteen Bahamians in Bimini, Bahamas, about sixty miles off the coast of Miami. Just before it was time for me to preach we were all on our knees in prayer. I had not decided what to preach on. But, in a flash, I had an unusual leading to preach on Hebrews 13:8: "Jesus Christ is the same yesterday and today and for ever." In that moment it was *almost* as though I could see the person of Jesus. He was so real to me for several minutes. And what was brought home to me in great power was that one of the meanings of Hebrews 13:8 is that *he looks the same*. His face is the same. But more than that, he still has the nail prints in his hands as he showed himself to Thomas several days after his resurrection from the dead (John 20:27). The man Jesus is the same yesterday, today and for ever. But when I preached that evening I was given the greatest anointing I think I have ever had. Why? You tell me. I only know that I was able to make clear what I have just shared here – only more so and in greater power. Those nineteen Bahamians never forgot it. I have preached there since, but they all remember that one particular evening when I spoke on Hebrews 13:8.

We are all curious as to what Jesus looked like. But

35

Isaiah tells us something that we must never forget: his appearance was lacklustre. It was nondescript. "He had no beauty or majesty to attract us to him, nothing in his appearance that we should desire him." This gives a fairly strong hint that he is not the handsome, good-looking Hollywood-like star that he is depicted as in some portraits – like that by Warner Sallman (1892–1968), whose famous "Head of Christ" is one of the best-known American portraits of the twentieth century. I doubt Jesus looked "presidential", had the bearing of a prince, or was bubbling over with charisma.

But you can be sure of one thing: he had an anointing of the Holy Spirit. We also know the effect he had on people. On one occasion the chief priests and Pharisees ordered the temple guards to arrest Jesus. They returned shortly afterwards – but without Jesus. "Why didn't you bring him in?" They could only reply: "No one ever spoke the way this man does" (John 7:45–46). It was the anointing. An amazing effect. There was no natural explanation for it. Indeed, Jesus had an unparalleled, unsurpassable and unprecedented anointing of the Holy Spirit. "God anointed Jesus of Nazareth with the Holy Spirit and power, and how he went around doing good and healing all who were under the power of the devil, because God was with him" (Acts 10:38). The word "Messiah" means "anointed". The word "Christ" comes from the Greek root *chrio* which means smearing as with an ointment. Both words – Messiah or Christ – mean the "anointed one".

On one occasion, in a synagogue in Nazareth, Jesus was handed the scroll of the prophet Isaiah. Unrolling it, he found the place where it was written:

The Spirit of the Lord is on me, because he has anointed me to preach good news to the poor. He has sent me to proclaim freedom for the prisoners and recovery of sight for the blind, to release the oppressed, to proclaim the year of the Lord's favour.

(LUKE 4:18–19; CF. ISAIAH 61:1–2)

Note that Jesus himself looked for and "found the place where it is written" (Luke 4:17), and then, after reading it, said: "Today this scripture is fulfilled in your hearing" (Luke 4:21). This was Jesus' way of saying that this passage referred to himself. In other words he was saying: "This is me. This describes me. This is all about me." I wish I could say the people were thrilled that one from their home town would be the promised Messiah. But no. They tried to get rid of him, then and there (Luke 4:28–29). In any case, Jesus was anointed by the Spirit to preach the good news to the poor and to set people free. He had an anointing "with the oil of joy" (Hebrews 1:9; Psalm 45:7). But, as he put it elsewhere: "Only in his home town and in his own house is a prophet without honour" (Matthew 13:57).

There are two generally accepted facts concerning the Messiah who was promised to Israel. These facts could be labelled *the dream* and *the reality*. First, the dream: the

Messiah was to be the hope of Israel – all that they ever wished for. He would put Israel on the map and exalt that nation above all others. Second, the reality: the Messiah was rejected by Israel – his own people. This is what Isaiah 53 is all about – how God's chosen, covenant people rejected the very Messiah they were looking forward to. Isaiah saw it seven hundred years in advance. The moment he said "he had no beauty or majesty to attract us to him", you could tell where Isaiah was going. He saw it coming. It was heavy on his heart. It was as though he was thinking: "Nobody is going to like this." It was not what he wanted to report. The promised Messiah would not be accepted by Israel because he did not measure up to what they wanted.

The Old Testament is full of predictions that the Messiah would definitely come. It is also full of descriptions of what he would be like. The Jews were also full of anticipation. They eagerly desired their Messiah to show up. The problem was that they were so selective with the various passages of Scripture that they built their hopes on their *dream* – verses that appealed to them. They fancied another David, another Solomon, another magnificent temple, another Moses – a charismatic, military leader who would have such undoubted authority and authenticity that all would instantly recognize him. He would overthrow Rome. No more would Jews have to bear the sight of Roman soldiers in their country. The Messiah would rid the nation of these unwelcome men. No one could possibly miss the Messiah!

But they were wrong. To begin with, this same person

who would "sprinkle many nations" (Isaiah 52:15) was almost unrecognizable, said Isaiah. He was "like a root out of dry ground" (Isaiah 53:1) – something you would hardly notice.

By the way, we all are vulnerable to the same thing that bedeviled ancient Israel: being selective with biblical verses that, in our anticipation, point to God's "next move on the earth". We fancy that we know what it will be like. When I used to travel to Wales (one of my favorite places), I often got the feeling that some of the people there felt they were in a better position than most to know what "true revival" was like. After all, the Welsh Revival (1904–05) was a phenomenon that led to many thousands of people being converted. And yet it was different from previous awakenings. Neither has there been anything like it since. We need to be knowledgable of all the awakenings of the Spirit in ancient history – going back to Enoch (Genesis 5:21; Hebrews 11:5). God has many precedents in history to choose from, and yet he might choose to do what has never been done before, as Elijah found out (1 Kings 19:11–13). Furthermore, not one single person described in Hebrews 11 – the chapter of the great people of faith – had the luxury of repeating the examples of a previous generation. But the better we know the Word of God, the less likely it will be that we should miss what God is up to next.

I will never forget a letter I received from a London minister during the time we were making certain changes in Westminster Chapel. We began singing choruses (as well as hymns), going out onto the streets to give out the Pilot Light tracts and a gentle appeal for people to confess Christ openly. This had not been done before. This London minister (also a friend) wrote: "R. T., when revival comes to London I'll know it!" Whew! A little rebuke from an old friend. And yet would he know it? We are all so sure that we would recognize the authentic when it arrives. You could not have told a Sadducee or a Pharisee that the Messiah would come to Israel without them knowing and acknowledging him. But he came and they rejected him.

We must never forget that the whole Bible is inspired by the Holy Spirit – it is infallible. This means we cannot be selective in our determination of which parts to believe and which are more appealing to us. It is a common habit – we have all done this – to go to Scripture with our own prejudices in order to find support for what we have chosen to believe. It is hard not to do this. But we must labour to avoid this. Otherwise we may miss something extremely important, profound, and strategic. Despising the "day of small things" (Zechariah 4:10) can even include overlooking a verse in the Bible that we may not fancy. I was once interviewed by the BBC World Service. They wanted to do a programme on "Heaven and Hell". Apparently they looked high and low over London for someone who believed in Hell as much as in Heaven. They got word about me and asked: "Do you really believe in Hell?" "Yes," I said, and reminded them that it was Jesus who had the most to say about the subject. We can so easily miss truth in the Bible – and overlook what

God may want to do in our time.

As for me, I do not want to miss any work of God on this planet, neither do I want to overlook any verse in the Word of God. All Scripture is inspired and each verse has its purpose – even if some are more important than others. And yet what was true of Jesus was told in advance.

The Jews, then, speaking generally, did not consider that Isaiah 53 referred to what the Messiah would look like and how he would be rejected by the very people he was promised to. Even some of Jesus' own disciples did not accept for a while some of the things he taught and foretold – such as his own crucifixion and resurrection. Jesus said that he must be killed and, on the third day, be raised to life. "Never, Lord!" said Peter. Jesus replied: "Get behind me, Satan! You are a stumbling block to me" (Matthew 16:22). Jesus said again to his disciples: "The Son of Man is going to be betrayed into the hands of men. They will kill him, and on the third day he will be raised to life." Their reaction: "the disciples were filled with grief" (Matthew 17:22–23). We all tend to affirm what we want to hear and allow other truths to bring us down – or let painful things go in one ear and out the other.

Isaiah saw the Messiah's vulnerability in advance. "He grew up before him like a tender shoot." A tender plant is so fragile. Isaiah was actually showing reasons one would not *naturally* believe in Israel's Messiah. The Jews never conceived of a need to accept their Messiah by "faith". That was not on their radar screen. They thought his presence and stature would be self-evident. But neither was Isaiah trying to "sell" anyone; that is, he was not trying to convince anybody to believe him. Consider, for example, when you go into a store to look around at various products. The salesperson will try to convince you to buy this or that. Isaiah was not doing that. If anything, he was putting us off. What is impressive about a plant so fragile? Indeed, a plant like that could be stepped on, dismissed, or never seen. Not only did the Virgin Mary carry the seed in her womb for nine months, Joseph and Mary had to flee from Herod's wrath – going to Egypt to protect the child (Matthew 2:13ff). Imagine having to go to such pains to protect God's Messiah and only Son!

Isaiah also saw in advance that the Messiah would show little promise and even be barely noticeable. "A root out of dry ground." Who would notice such a thing? A root in moist soil would have promise – and grow quickly. It would soon flourish. A root out of dry ground would surely become nothing in a short period of time. A root out of dry ground would be vulnerable, fragile, and unpromising. It would have no future. What kind of future does a man hanging on a cross have? What kind of expectation does a man with no charisma have? A person who is charismatic usually has a strong personality. Israel's Messiah would be a prophet like Moses (Deuteronomy 18:15) – a strong figure indeed. But Jesus so blended in with the crowd that Judas Iscariot had to arrange a signal with the chief priests and elders: "The one I kiss is the man; arrest him," he said to them (Matthew 26:48). Jesus let them arrest him (Matthew 26:50). He appeared helpless instead of being strong.

The Messiah's appearance, then, was possibly the greatest disappointment of all. There was "nothing in his appearance that we should desire him". We all like our leaders to "look the part" – that is, to give the aura of excellence, dignity, and prestige. So what a disappointment Jesus was. He was no Moses! He was no David! He was no Solomon! Yes, thousands were going to make him king after he fed them with two fish and five loaves of bread (John 6:15), but right after then his teaching put them utterly off. Telling the crowd that they must eat his flesh and drink his blood was not the politically correct thing to do. And when he preached the sovereignty of God – "No one can come to me unless the Father has enabled him" – that did it: "From this time many of his disciples turned back and no longer followed him" (John 6:65–66). He had no appearance that made people want to follow him in the first place, but his teaching ensured that the thousands dwindled to a handful.

The truth is, Jesus was a prophet like Moses. He was the offspring of David. He had a greater wisdom than Solomon. Indeed, Jesus fitted every single prophetic word that preceded him. But little lines such as "root out of dry ground" or "nothing in his appearance that we should desire him" were overlooked by the Jews of the day. The result: Israel as a whole missed its Messiah. How often had rabbis read from Isaiah 64:1: "Oh, that you would rend the heavens and come down"? That verse was read in every synagogue in Judea and Galilee. But when he came down from Heaven – and was right under their noses – they missed God's Messiah entirely. It is so sad.

The Jews honestly thought that the Messiah would be instantly recognizable, immensely popular, and impossible not to notice. There were occasional incidents which prompted people to "jump on the bandwagon" – such as in John 6:15, and when the crowds shouted "Hosanna!" on Palm Sunday (Matthew 21:9) – but Jesus himself did not let such movements get off the ground. On Palm Sunday, as soon as he entered Jerusalem, instead of announcing his kingship to the governmental authorities, he went to the temple mount and overthrew the money changers (Matthew 21:12). Again, that was not the politically correct thing to do.

That aforementioned verse, "Who despises the day of small things?" (Zechariah 4:10), may therefore refer to insignificant verses in the Bible as well as insignificant days. It should teach us a lesson never to underestimate the importance of any verse in the Word of God. Spiritual discernment should not only help us to recognize verses that many suppose are unimportant but also help us to see the presence of God when we think he is not there. "Surely the Lord is in this place, and I was not aware of it," said Jacob (Genesis 28:16). True spiritual maturity should enable one to close the time gap between the occasion of God's presence and the moment we perceive it. The Messiah was present before the very eyes of Israel, and only a few perceived him eventually. But one day "every knee will bow" and "every tongue confess" who Jesus is (Romans 14:11; Philippians 2:9–11).

True, we are also curious about what Jesus looked like. But there were no cameras, no artists. We don't know if he was tall or short, had brown hair or black hair. There is an ancient tradition that Jesus was blond! Some portraits of Jesus show him with a halo over his head. And yet he had distinctive features. No doubt he looked something like his mother, but no one knows what she looked like. If he looked partly like his mother and partly like his father, how would the likeness of Jesus' Father show up? If Adam was created after God's own likeness, perhaps Jesus looked partly like his mother and partly the way God made Adam. But that is sheer speculation!

One thing is certain: we shall all see him one day. You will see him. Every person who ever lived will see him. All people – saved or lost – will see him. This is because "every eye" shall see him when he comes in his glory. Those who are lost will weep and wail because of him (Revelation 1:7). It may be like what John saw when kings of the earth, princes, generals, the rich and the mighty hid in caves and among the rocks of the mountains. They called to the mountains and the rocks: "Fall on us and hide us from the face of him who sits on the throne and from the wrath of the Lamb!" (Revelation 6:15–16). It won't matter what he looks like then. But it will be a long way from being a "tender shoot".

I am fascinated by that moment when a detachment

of soldiers and officials from the chief priests came looking for Jesus with Judas Iscariot. Jesus asked them: "Who is it you want?" It is obvious that they did not have a clue it was him! He replied: "I am he." In that moment, dozens of soldiers "drew back and *fell to* the *ground*" (John 18:4–6). That brief occasion is a hint of the kind of power Jesus had. If the sound of his voice when they saw him had that kind of effect, think how easily Jesus could have intervened in all the plans of his enemies to achieve instant vindication. But he never wanted vindication; he came to do the Father's will – to be rejected and to die on a cross for our sins.

There are two kinds of vindication: internal and external. External vindication is when others clear your name and exonerate you from any sense of guilt or blame. It is when your name is openly cleared. Internal vindication is when you have it in your heart; that is, when you have sufficient confidence that you have got it right and don't need external vindication. This internal vindication is exactly what Jesus had from the days of his baptism to his death on the cross. This is why Paul said that Jesus was "vindicated by the Spirit" (1 Timothy 3:16). In other words, the immediate and direct witness of the Spirit was sufficient for Jesus while he was on this earth. His external vindication will come after his Second Coming, when every knee shall bow and every tongue confess that he is God Almighty in the flesh (Philippians 2:9–11; Romans 14:10).

There are also two comings of Jesus. Isaiah 53 is about Jesus' First Coming. That was two thousand years ago. It was the First Coming that required faith in order to see who he was. Not many believed this message; the arm of the Lord was not revealed to a vast number of people. But at the Second Coming there will be no faith required; all people who ever lived will see and know him then. There will be no need to point him out, there will be no one needing to say "it is the one I kiss". However, your reaction to the Second Coming will be determined by your reaction to his First Coming. If you recognize Jesus' First Coming through preaching you will be among those who will be ecstatic with indescribable joy at his Second Coming. But if you reject his First Coming you will be among those who weep and wail at his Second Coming.

This need not happen to you. As you read these lines you may thank God that the Second Coming is still in the future (although I will tell you that I am one who believes he is coming soon). If you embrace the Gospel that is being taught in this very book it means you will rejoice when Jesus comes a second time. God did not try to make Jesus attractive in his First Coming – by his appearance or his death. His glory was veiled in human flesh – and an unimpressive figure at that. God did not want people believing in his Son because he was made attractive to the human eye but because by faith people believed the "message", the "report", because the arm of the Lord made them see it.

Therefore Jesus started life as a helpless baby – like everyone else. People expected him to be born in Bethlehem. Every young woman in Bethlehem grew up hoping she

would be the mother of God's Messiah. But his parents were
Nazarenes and only came to Bethlehem because of certain
Roman laws regarding taxes (Luke 2:1–7). Nobody living at
the time would have predicted that this was the way Scripture
would be fulfilled. As we saw above, the child Jesus needed
to be protected by his parents in his early days (Matthew
2:13–23). Nobody dreamed he would be brought up in a
place like Nazareth. Indeed, he was brought up in a town
regarded as the least likely to produce greatness. That is the
reputation Nazareth had. When it came to prestige, Galilee
generally was always regarded as beneath Judea (Isaiah 9:1),
and Nazareth was the least esteemed of all cities in Galilee.
"Nazareth! Can anything good come from there?" Nathanael
asked (John 1:46). Even when he chose his disciples, Jesus
picked people that impressed no one. He chose a tax collector
and fishermen – not those who had an impeccable pedigree
or reputation. In other words, his following quite mirrored
his own appearance: there was nothing "attractive" about
him or them! He might have started at the top – with Herod,
priests, religious authorities, Pharisees, and Sadducees. But
no, he started virtually at the bottom – with those who had
no great education or background.

Jesus even made sure that his miracles did not compete
with his essential glory. As soon as he had fed five thousand
men with the loaves and fish, he preached the most offensive
kind of message you can imagine. He did not want people
following him for the material benefits he could offer them;
he wanted them to see he was the bread of life that came

down from the Father (John 6:51) and that his following was comprised of those given to him by the Father (John 6:37). God ordained the entire scenario of Jesus' First Coming so that people would accept his Son based on the message he preached, not on the charismatic power he was able to demonstrate. They would accept his Son by *faith*. "Who has believed our message and to whom has the arm of the Lord been revealed?" Isaiah saw all of this seven hundred years before it happened.

Certainly there *are* subsidiary benefits that come from following Christ. King David saw this one thousand years before Christ's coming: "Praise the Lord, O my soul, and forget not all his benefits – who forgives all your sins and heals all your diseases, who redeems your life from the pit and crowns you with love and compassion, who satisfies your desires with good things so that your youth is renewed like the eagle's" (Psalm 103:2–5). Yes, there are benefits – wonderful, glorious blessings – that come to those who hear the Saviour's voice. But these blessings come to those who embrace Christ for who he was and what he did, dying on a cross for our sins. God wants us to love him as he is. The happiest thing a wife or husband can hear from their spouse is: "I love you as you are." And God wants us to love him and his Son *just as he is*. We all have imperfections for our loved ones to overlook. But God has no imperfections. The more you know him, the more you love him; the longer you serve him, the more you revere and respect him.

God could have done it another way. When Paul said

that in God's "wisdom" it was determined that his people would be saved by the "foolishness of what is preached", the obvious implication is that God had other options. He might have chosen to save people according to their wisdom. If so, how many would be saved? What if he chose to save people according to their knowledge? Would you be happy with that? What if he chose those who are royal, noble, upper class, cultured, and educated? How many would be saved? In other words, God had options, but he chose to bypass all but one: to save those who "believe" by the foolishness of what is preached – the death of his Son on a cross.

Can you live with this? Will you believe this? Will you confess him? Don't be ashamed of him. If you are ashamed of him he will be ashamed of you. But if you confess Jesus Christ before all people, the Father will acknowledge you and affirm you (Matthew 10:32). You will be adopted into his family and made a son or daughter of our Heavenly Father forever.

Martin Luther called John 3:16 "the Bible in a nutshell": "For God so loved the world that he gave his one and only Son, that whoever believes in him shall not perish but have eternal life." Luther also said he was so glad that this verse did not say: "God so loved Martin Luther that if Martin Luther believed Martin Luther would have eternal life." Why? Luther replied: "It could have referred to *another* Martin Luther." But Jesus said that God so loved the "world" that "whoever believes" may have eternal life. That lets you and me in. That also means we are without excuse.

CHAPTER THREE

The Man Who Knew Rejection

> He was despised and rejected by men, a man
> of sorrows, and familiar with suffering. Like
> one from whom men hide their faces he was
> despised, and we esteemed him not.
>
> ISAIAH 53:3

I will never forget a question an old friend, who had just gone through the trauma of a terrible divorce, put to me a few years ago: "R. T., have you any idea what it is like to experience utter rejection, when there is no self-esteem left?" I don't believe I have. I felt that day as if I myself had not suffered rejection at all. I only barely know what it is to be given the "silent treatment", to be isolated, treated with a measure of contempt, or to be set to one side by people who formerly had affirmed me. The way some people are rejected today is not by physical pain; they are merely "put into perspective", to quote the poet Steve Turner. And that hurts. But my experience is mild when compared to that of others – perhaps your own.

Rejection is the feeling of abandonment. The word "rejection" apparently dates back to 1415. The original meaning means "to throw back". To reject means to send back, to refuse to accept, or to refuse to believe in. It means to be deserted. Social rejection, or personal rejection, is when a person is deliberately excluded from an interpersonal relationship. Peer rejection – when a person is intentionally disregarded by people of their own age, class, school, background, culture or affiliation, or even their family – is similar. But possibly the worst thing of all is to be rejected by one's own parents.

In 1970, I was privileged to take a course in counselling at the Narramore Christian Foundation in Rosemead, California. While the purpose of the course was to help me to counsel others, the immediate result was that it changed my own life. The founder of this institution, Dr Clyde Narramore, adopted as his slogan: "Every person is worth understanding." This shrewd and profound phrase suggested not only that each person deserves to understand himself or herself but also that others deserve to be understood before we judge them. In other words, if we knew more about the background of a person whom we are ready to judge, we might lower our voices and be sympathetic. If we could see into the other person's hurts, suffering, situation, and lack of opportunity, we would almost certainly be less likely to point the finger and throw the book at someone we may find unappealing.

One of the most common causes of undesirable behaviour or of having a strange personality is rejection. Being rejected can have severe repercussions on one's psychological profile. For example, when a person has been rejected by an authority figure – a parent, relative, school teacher, or church leader – the emotional consequences can be horrendous. This is to say nothing of being rejected by one's spouse, or being jilted by someone you loved.

One Saturday morning in London, one of our Pilot Lights, Margaret Paddon, observed a man called Michael sitting on the pavement behind the Army & Navy Store in Victoria Street. She offered him a tract. He refused it. She lovingly and patiently continued to talk with him. He replied that God did not want him and he did not want God. Margaret asked him why he felt this way. It turned out that he had been brought up in a foster home and was later rejected by his foster parents. He was thrown out of his home. As a teenager he began to live rough. But he decided one day to look up his natural parents, hoping they would be glad to see him. The moment he showed up they slammed the door in his face and ordered him never to come back. You might call this a triple rejection. Margaret pleaded with him to come to Westminster Chapel on the following Sunday, promising that she would sit with him if he came. He did. Week after week he sat with Mr and Mrs Paddon during our Sunday services. In the meantime, he was converted. I baptized him. He became the first member of the Chapel to be converted through our Pilot Light ministry. He got a job and found a place to live. He was a lovely man. But he also had a heart condition. My last memory of him was seeing him in the grey suit he bought for himself and wore every Sunday. He died while having open heart surgery. And yet we would have never met him if Margaret Paddon had not offered to be friendly to him. His acute sense of rejection had isolated him from the world. He was worth understanding.

Are you a person who has suffered by being rejected? Perhaps you never got over that girlfriend or boyfriend who jilted you. Perhaps it was a teacher. A boss. An old friend. Maybe you were rejected merely because of the colour of your skin. Perhaps you were rejected for a job, or a promotion. Rejection has possibly left a scar that has shaped your perspective, your self-image, and your hope for any kind of happy life.

Jesus of Nazareth was a man who knew rejection. What he went through was horrible – from sibling rivalry to the cross. The cross not only meant rejection by his own people but, as we will see, the ultimate rejection, namely, by his Father. "He was despised and rejected by men, a man of sorrows, and familiar with suffering."

Why is Jesus' suffering important for you and me? It is mainly because he was achieving salvation for us but also because he totally sympathizes with our own sense of rejection. Perhaps all of us have suffered rejection to some degree, but none of us will ever face rejection as Jesus did.

What is more, he never forgot it. You and I may go through an ordeal, then get over it and forget about it. Jesus never did that. Although he is now at the right hand of God, Jesus has never forgotten what it was like to be rejected. That is where you and I come in. Jesus is the Great Sympathizer.

The New Testament teaches us that, after Jesus died on the cross, he "sat down at the right hand" of God (Hebrews 1:3). Whereas the priests of the Old Testament fulfilled their calling while on this earth – and carried out their duties always *standing* – Jesus became a priest after he died and ascended to Heaven – and sat down! The writer of the epistle to the Hebrews also gave Jesus a title not found elsewhere in the Bible: high priest (Hebrews 4:14). The high priest, or chief priest, was the highest ranking priest in ancient times. His greatest responsibility was to go into the Most Holy Place on the Day of Atonement to make atonement for the people. He was always chosen from the tribe of Levi. But Jesus was from the tribe of Judah (Hebrews 7:14), so how could he be called a priest? It was because of another Old Testament prophecy, Psalm 110:4: "You are a priest for ever, in the order of Melchizedek." Jesus fulfilled that prophetic word.

The writer of the epistle to the Hebrews compared Jesus to the priests of the Old Testament. The ancient priests were not able to sympathize with those for whom they made atonement through animal sacrifices. This was because they were preoccupied with their meticulous responsibility to get the ceremonial law carried out to perfection. The feelings of the people did not cross their minds; they only thought of their prescribed duties as priests. In the person of Jesus we do not have a high priest like that, but instead one "who has been tempted in every way, just as we are – yet was without sin" (Hebrews 4:15). I love the Authorized Version translation, that Jesus is "touched with the feeling" of our infirmities. The ancient priest was never touched with feeling for his fellow Israelites. But Jesus was – and is. At this moment. He feels for us and feels with us in our sense of pain and rejection.

Isaiah tells us that Jesus was "despised". Why? Why would a man who spent his time loving people, instructing people and healing people be despised? Surely he would be a hero! He might have been such. But his teaching and his claims were so offensive that they overruled any chance of being Israel's hero in his day. As long as he was feeding the people miraculously with the loaves and fish, they were thrilled; indeed, they wanted to make him king (John 6:15). But his teaching became so offensive that they completely forgot about making him king and deserted him right, left and centre!

What caused the people to despise Jesus? As I explained above, it was partly his looks – his appearance both in life and death. There was "nothing in his appearance" that Jews would desire him. Instead of "looking the part" (in America, it is called looking "presidential"), he simply did not have the charisma to mesmerize people at the natural level. But there is more. When Pontius Pilate said to the crowds who demanded his crucifixion, "Here is your king" (John 19:14), it was a way of making light of Jesus' appearance. Pilate loved to stick the knife into the hearts of the Jews whenever he could. So he pretended that he believed this was their king! Jesus had a crown of thorns put on his head, and a purple robe showing royalty put on him to wear (John 19:2). Pilate knew that Jesus' appearance was disgusting to those who were looking for a charismatic military leader to be the Messiah.

But what truly offended the Jews was Jesus' teaching, and the deity he claimed for himself. Referring to the manna in the wilderness in Moses' day, Jesus actually said to the Jews that he was the "bread of God" that "comes down from heaven and gives life to the world" (John 6:33). To show their disapproval at this language they immediately referred to rumours abroad that Jesus was born illegitimately, something they were prepared to overlook as long as he was feeding them. But when he said, "I am the bread that came down from heaven," they retorted: "Is this not Jesus, the son of Joseph, whose father and mother we know?" (John 6:41–42).

And yet that was only the beginning. He looked at the crowds and pointed out to them that not a single one of them could come to him unless God drew them to him (John 6:44). That put them in their place. But there was more. Since he was the "living bread that came down from heaven", such bread being his "flesh", he said to them all: "Unless you can eat the flesh of the Son of Man and drink his blood, you have no life in you. Whoever eats my flesh and drinks my blood has eternal life, and I will raise him up at the last day" (John 6:53–54). Their response to this was to say: "This is a hard teaching. Who can accept it?" (John 6:60). The consequence was that "from this time many of his disciples turned back and no longer followed him" (John 6:66).

Jesus claimed that all he said and did was being orchestrated in Heaven by his Father. "I tell you the truth, the Son can do nothing by himself; he can do only what he sees his Father doing, because whatever the Father does the Son also does" (John 5:19). Furthermore, "By myself I can do nothing; I judge only as I hear, and my judgment is just, for I seek not to please myself but him who sent me" (John 5:30). All his teaching added up to one thing: that Jesus was God. They got the message, that "he was even calling God his own Father, making himself equal with God" (John 5:18). Later on, when they picked up stones to stone him, they said to him that they were not stoning him for his miracles, "but for blasphemy, because you, a mere man, claim to be God" (John 10:33). When Jesus said to a paralytic, "Son your sins are forgiven," they said: "He's blaspheming! Who can forgive sins but God alone?" (Mark 2:5–7). Quite. Jesus *was* God the Son and the Son of God. "For God so loved the world that he gave his one and only Son, that whoever believes in him shall not perish but have eternal life" (John 3:16).

And yet the way he died in the end was the final straw. "Like one from whom men hide their faces he was despised, and we esteemed him not." They reasoned that if Jesus really were God's Messiah he could not be crucified – God would not allow it. Muslims reason in much the same way; that a true prophet could not be crucified; therefore Allah delivered Jesus from the cross. But this is why the Gospel is so offensive and why the devil hates the blood of Jesus Christ. All enemies of Jesus Christ will seek to dismiss the cross of Christ. The appearance of Jesus hanging on a cross was so despicable, so off-putting, and so horrifying that, says Isaiah, the Jews could not bear to look at him. I think of the old spiritual, "Were you there when they crucified my Lord?" Indeed, the thought of it all causes one to tremble. Tremble. Tremble.

However, the whole scenario of Jesus' rejection continued after his death – and continues to this day. I refer to the way he was and is revealed in the proclamation of the Gospel. The very notion that people would receive the Messiah through "the foolishness of what was preached" (1 Corinthians 1:21) was so beneath their dignity that all who represented Jesus would be hated as much as he was. Jesus actually forecast this too: "If the world hates you, keep in mind that it hated me first" (John 15:18).

To summarize: the Jews despised Jesus because of his appearance, his teaching, his death, and the way he would be accepted. The Messiah would only be accepted by faith alone. Your good works won't help you. In fact your good works could hurt! How? If you think they help! This means you and I can only be saved through his very performance on our behalf. Jesus did it all by his life (keeping the Law) and his death (atoning for our sins). It was a magnificent performance. It was brilliant. And when he uttered those words, "It is finished" (John 19:30), the Father agreed that it was brilliant. That was when the veil of the temple – which separated the outer court from the holy of holies – was torn in two from top to bottom, showing that only God could do this (Matthew 27:51).

Isaiah also says that Jesus was distressed. Distress refers to anguish of mind. There was more than one reason Jesus experienced distress. For one thing, he saw the injustices of this world as no man saw them. If you think *you* see what is unjust and unfair in this world, your powers of observation are not to be compared with what Jesus saw. All the thoughts you and I may have about why God allows suffering were intensified a thousand times more in Jesus' perception. One of the reasons God became man is so that you and I can be sure that God was represented by one who sees all the suffering of the world. Does God notice injustice? Yes, infinitely more than you and I do. And Jesus is the proof of this. Jesus experienced sorrow and distress as you and I will never experience them. And he that has seen Jesus has seen the Father (John 14:9). This is one of the reasons God sent his Son into the world.

As to the answer to the question, "Why does God allow evil and suffering when he has the power to stop it", I reply: one day God will clear his name. He will do it *then*. We do it *now*. The difference between the Christian and the non-

Christian is this: the true believer vindicates God now. The non-Christian will experience God vindicating himself on the Last Day. But there will be no opportunity for true faith by then. But as for suffering and evil, Jesus saw it all and showed his concern all the time.

Jesus' attention was diverted on one occasion by a widow whose only son had died. His body was being carried out. When Jesus saw this woman his heart went out to her. He said to her, "Don't cry," then raised the young man from the dead (Luke 7:13–15). If you are hurting as you read these lines – perhaps you have been in tears owing to what you have been put through – Jesus says to you: "Don't cry." He notices. This is what caused him to be distressed when he was on this earth. He was fully aware of all the suffering around him. And at God's right hand he is still "touched with feeling" when he sees your pain.

Jesus suffered but never complained. He never gave into self-pity. He never had the "Elijah complex" (1 Kings 19:10). He never said of the Pharisees: "These men don't appreciate me as they should. They don't see what I am capable of doing for them." Jesus never gave into that. He never wore his pain on his sleeve. This is where many of us fail. If you are like me, it is hard to suffer without some kind of murmuring or grumbling accompanying that hurt. It is also important to be able never to take on rejection; that is, to let past rejection set you up for imaginary situations. That would be having a rejection complex – which Elijah had. It is one thing, then, to be rejected; it is another thing to anticipate it and be governed by what you fear might happen. It is also important not to impute to another person that they should treat you with more respect than they do. "I am able to do more than people recognize in me," we may be tempted to think or say. We should make Jesus our model. Nobody – ever – felt rejection as he did; but he never called attention to it.

And yet he experienced agony as he anticipated the cross. His greatest fear came from what he anticipated when going to the cross. In the Garden of Gethsemane he experienced anguish and loneliness. He hoped the disciples – that is, at least, his inner circle – would stand by him in his darkest hour. He took Peter, James and John with him to Gethsemane, and said to them: "My soul is overwhelmed with sorrow to the point of death. Stay here and keep watch with me" (Matthew 26:38). This was one of the most transparent, candid and vulnerable statements Jesus ever made. He was confiding in his closest friends. How would you feel if our Lord confided in you like that? "The Lord confides in those who fear him" (Psalm 25:14). I cannot wish for a greater privilege than for the Lord to confide in me like that. But if the disciples twigged, they hardly showed it. Jesus prayed: "My Father, if it is possible, may this cup be taken from me. Yet not as I will, but as you will" (Matthew 26:39). Luke's account tells us that an angel from Heaven appeared to him and strengthened him (Luke 22:43). I think we can infer from this that when our friends abandon us God will send an angel to take their place. God knows when we need an angel.

There is more: "being in anguish, he prayed more earnestly, and his sweat was like drops of blood falling to the ground" (Luke 22:44). The disciples slept through the entire ordeal. Yes, they slept. He pleaded with them: "Could you men not keep watch with me for one hour?" They kept on sleeping. Jesus gave up hoping to have them with him when he was entering the most difficult moment ever a man experienced. He simply said to them: "Sleep on now, and take your rest" (Matthew 26:45, AV). He now knew conclusively that he would go to the cross totally alone.

I grew up in Kentucky singing this chorus:

Standing somewhere in the shadows you'll
    find Jesus;
He's the only one who cares and understands;
Standing somewhere in the shadows you'll
    find Jesus,
And you'll know him by the nail prints in his hands.

(ANON)

I mentioned how Jesus experienced rejection by his siblings. His half-brothers were apparently very jealous of him. John records an unhappy incident when Jesus' brothers said to him: "You ought to leave here and go to Judea, so that your disciples may see the miracles you do. No one who wants to become a public figure acts in secret. Since you are doing these things, show yourself to the world". Jesus was never trying to be a "public figure". But it was a way of their making him appear that way, putting him down and dismissing him as an ambitious person who was trying to make a name for himself. It must have hurt. John added, "For even his own brothers did not believe in him" (John 7:2–5). Young David, before he was king, experienced the same thing. "I know how conceited you are," his brother Eliab said to him (1 Samuel 17:28).

Many great people have known rejection. Charles Spurgeon (1834–92) was rejected by Regent's Park College (my old college, after it moved from London to Oxford). G. Campbell Morgan (1863–1945), former minister of Westminster Chapel, was rejected by the Methodist Church. They said he did not have the makings of a preacher. A young man tried out for the choir at the First Assemblies of God in Memphis, Tennessee, a number of years ago. He was turned down. They said he did not have a good voice. His name was Elvis Presley.

When Jesus came down from the Mount of Olives on Palm Sunday, the crowds cheered. They shouted: "Hosanna to the Son of David! Blessed is he who comes in the name of the Lord! Hosanna in the highest!" (Matthew 21:9). The people somehow thought Jesus was then going to declare himself God's Messiah, reveal himself as the military leader Israel was awaiting, and – presently – overthrow Rome. When Jesus entered Jerusalem he made a left turn – to the temple – and overthrew the money changers. A right turn would have meant he would confront the Roman authorities. The left turn directed him where his followers did not anticipate. After Gethsemane came his betrayal by Judas Iscariot. This fulfilled an ancient psalm: "Even my close friend, whom I trusted, he who shared my bread, has lifted up his heel against me" (Psalm 41:9). He was then arrested. "Then all the disciples deserted him and fled" (Matthew 26:56). Rejection. Where were those men when he needed them? Where were those who were healed? Where were those who witnessed Lazarus being raised from the dead? They all deserted him.

Jesus is depicted by Isaiah as a "man of sorrows". He was the embodiment of suffering. He lived with inner pain. The burden of the entire world was on him. Some people have read into this that Jesus never laughed. Or smiled. I have no idea whether he ever laughed. Since laughter is often making fun of someone, it is possible that he never laughed. Although I would not be surprised if he laughed a lot. I am quite sure he smiled. I can't prove it of course, but I have my reasons for believing he smiled.

He was a man of sorrows, and "acquainted with grief" (Isaiah 53:3, AV). Jesus of Nazareth was familiar with suffering. You don't need to know this sort of thing about Jesus when you are in a good mood, getting good reports, getting a rise in pay, getting an exciting invitation, feeling popular, having money to pay your bills, knowing no physical pain, experiencing no rejection or hurt. When you are on top – on the mountain – you don't think a lot about Jesus being a man of sorrows and acquainted with grief or suffering. But who is the first person you turn to when you are in trouble, have no money to pay your bills, feel physical pain, experience emotional problems, anxiety, depression, and feelings of abandonment? You turn to Jesus. This is why Jesus is known as a man of sorrows. It is for us.

> **Man of sorrows! What a name**
> **For the Son of God, who came**
> **Ruined sinners to reclaim.**
> **Hallelujah! what a Saviour!**

PHILIP P. BLISS (1838–76)

Jesus also felt the pain of what others thought about him. Never think that Jesus was impervious to the opinions of people. How could he be tempted at "all points" as we are (Hebrews 4:15, AV) if he never took notice of the negative things people said about him? No one is so spiritual that he or she reaches the place where one does not feel the hurt of an unkind comment, unfair criticism (or fair criticism), or uncomplimentary remarks or words intended to inflict pain. We all love praise, and hate criticism. Somerset Maugham (1874–1965) said that when people ask for criticism they really want praise. We are all like that.

Although Jesus did not have a rejection complex, he felt the agony of the cross in advance. That is what Gethsemane was all about. And the fact that Isaiah saw Israel's Messiah as a "man of sorrows" seven hundred years in advance is proof that God knows the future. A scary thought this, that God knows where you and I will be one hundred years from now. He knows whether one will be in Heaven or Hell. The most important question you can ask yourself is: where will I be one hundred years from now? Do you know the answer to that question? You *can* know the answer to that question. I know the answer: I will be in Heaven. But you can know the same thing!

Nothing catches God by surprise. But there is an irony here: although God knows whether you will be in Heaven or Hell one hundred years from now, if you go to Heaven it will be by his sheer grace; if you go to Hell it will be your own fault. You do not need to go to Hell. You can go to Heaven – and know now that you are saved.

Jesus was a man of sorrows for you. He suffered for you. He was disgraced for you. It is no accident you are reading these words. It is because God is on your case. You are given fair warning of judgment to come. You can decide your case "out of court" – that is, make peace with your maker today.

I said above that Jesus continues to be despised by the way he is proclaimed; namely, through the very Gospel that permeates this book you are reading. He was repulsed by those who witnessed the cross. The sight was so horrid that we hid our faces from him, says Isaiah (53:3 in the AV). We got out of the picture. We did not want to be around him when he was deserted. Consider what it was like. Blood was oozing down from his forehead where the crown of thorns had been pressed on it, blood was still pouring from the scourging, blood came from his hands where the nails were put in and from his feet.

> **See, from His head, His hands, His feet,**
> **Sorrow and love flow mingled down;**
> **Did e'er such love and sorrow meet,**
> **Or thorns compose so rich a crown?**
>
> ISAAC WATTS (1674–1748)

And yet the worst thing of all came at an unexpected moment. Darkness came upon the earth. From approximately midday until three o'clock in the afternoon on Good Friday there was darkness and silence. Suddenly Jesus experienced the ultimate abandonment, desertion, and rejection. He cried out in Aramaic: *"Eloi, Eloi, lama sabachthani"* – "My God, my God, why have you forsaken me?" (Matthew 27:46). This was the hardest thing of all for Jesus to endure. I would opine that it was equally the hardest thing of all for the Father to endure. Jesus now felt the utter and total rejection of the Father. Never before had Jesus addressed the Father as God. He always addressed God as Father – always. But not here. He cried out: "My God, my God, why have you forsaken me?" It was one thing to experience the rejection of his siblings, the betrayal of Judas, the desertion of the twelve disciples; but to experience the abandonment of his Father was not calculated – not even in Gethsemane.

And yet this was the moment that he who knew no sin was made sin. This was the precise time when all our sins were laid on Jesus. Paul described it: "God made him who had no sin to be sin for us, so that in him we might become the righteousness of God" (2 Corinthians 5:21). This is a very important verse and one to which we will return in this book. It was an actual event that took place on this very planet some two thousand years ago, moments before Jesus died.

But that Jesus would cry out "Why?" suggests to me that God does not fault us when we too ask him: "Why?" We all ask: "Why?" It is not a sin to ask God: "Why?" "What is the reason for this Lord?" "What is the purpose of this?" "Why did you let this happen?" God does not mind this.

The big picture is that Jesus did this for us. It is the way he achieved our salvation. By suffering the rejection of the Father, he paid our debt of sin on the cross. But the smaller picture is that by suffering the abandonment of the Father he can sympathize with us when God hides his face and things happen which we do not understand.

What will you do with this information? Speaking for the way Israel would regard their Messiah, Isaiah said: "We esteemed him not." Sadly, he was right. But do you have to repeat the sin of ancient Israel? No! Instead of hiding your face from him you can esteem him. Affirm him. Bow to him. Do it today. Do it now. Do you know where you will be one hundred years from now? You can know. If from your heart you can pray the following words, you can be as saved as I am – or as the Apostle Paul was. We all have one hope: Jesus dying for us. Here is the prayer:

> Lord Jesus Christ, I need you. I want you. I am sorry for my sins. I know I cannot save myself. I renounce all hope in my good works. Wash my sins away by your blood. I welcome your Holy Spirit. As best as I know how, I give you my life. Amen.

CHAPTER FOUR

Who Crucified Jesus?

Surely he took up our infirmities and carried
our sorrows, yet we considered him stricken
by God, smitten by him, and afflicted.

ISAIAH 53:4

In 2004, I took Mel Gibson's film *The Passion of the Christ* into Ramalah, for Yasser Arafat (1929–2004) to see. He was interested in viewing the film, owing largely to the film's reputation of being anti-Semitic. It was thought that Gibson wanted to demonstrate that the Jews crucified Jesus. Arafat invited about thirty members of the Palestine Liberation Organization (PLO) to watch the film with us. To them, it was a demonstration not only that the Jews crucified Jesus but that they are doing the same thing to them.

The issue "Who crucified Jesus?" has always been a red-hot political and theological issue, especially in recent years. Many Jews feel it is unfair to them to say that the Jews crucified Jesus. For one thing, the Jews living today were not present at the crucifixion two thousand years ago. Secondly, anti-Semitism (a word that generally means hatred toward Jews) is often traced to the historical assumption that the Jews crucified Jesus. Jews today generally want to be let off the hook regarding this charge, and have resented the notion that Jews – then and now – should suffer from this accusation. The Vatican repudiated the deicide ("killing God") against the Jews in the Second Vatican Council document *Nostra Aetate* ("in our time").

The purpose of this chapter is not primarily to answer the historical or political question of who crucified Jesus, but to investigate Isaiah's words: "We considered him stricken by God, smitten by him, and afflicted." What did Isaiah mean by this? Answering this will necessarily bring us face to face with the teaching of the New Testament. My interest in any case is theological not political.

Could it be the devil?

What if I told you that Satan crucified Jesus? Could you accept this? For one thing, the devil knew all along who Jesus was. "What do you want with us, Jesus of Nazareth?" a demon cried to Jesus. "Have you come to destroy us? I know who you are – the Holy One of God!" (Mark 1:24). "What do you want with us, Son of God?... Have you come here to torture us before the appointed time?" (Matthew 8:29). The devil therefore knew who Jesus was but foolishly thought he could abort God's purpose in sending his Son into the world.

He therefore was at the bottom of a conspiracy to end the life of Jesus. According to John, Satan "prompted" Judas Iscariot to betray Jesus (John 13:2). According to Luke, Satan "entered" Judas Iscariot on the night he betrayed him (Luke 22:3). This means Judas was demon-possessed on the night he conspired with the authorities to hand Jesus over to them. How could a person who was with Jesus day and night for three years do such an evil thing? Answer: he was possessed by Satan. It is the only explanation. It also shows what people can do who listen to the devil. They are capable of the worst possible crimes.

Satan therefore thought that by destroying him, his arch-enemy Jesus would be completely out of the way and no longer a threat to his evil interests. The devil thought therefore he could control the world with Jesus dead. But Satan did not imagine that God might raise Jesus from the dead. That thought was not on the devil's radar screen. This also shows how Satan does not understand the Bible or he would not have made this miscalculation.

In any case, Satan had engineered the crucifixion of Jesus. What was "destined for our glory before time began", however, was utterly hidden from Satan. "None of the rulers of this age [that is, demonic powers] understood it [that is, God's ultimate purpose], for if they had, they would not have crucified the Lord of glory" (1 Corinthians 2:8). It is clear that: 1) the devil should be charged with having crucified Jesus; and, yet, 2) he never would have done this had he known that God would raise his Son from the dead!

So can Satan be charged with the crucifixion of Jesus? Yes.

Did God do it?

The people of Israel thought God did it: "we considered him stricken by God". According to Isaiah 53:4, the Jews believed God himself was behind the crucifixion of Jesus. Seven hundred years previously, Isaiah got into the skin of God's covenant people. He fully identified with the way they reasoned. God did it. "We considered him stricken by God." Enter into their thinking: "We [the covenant people of God] considered him [the Messiah] stricken by God [for blasphemy], smitten by him, and afflicted." Isaiah, by the Spirit, could see clearly the rationale that entered the minds of those who wanted the Messiah crucified. In three words: God did it. That was it – pure and simple: God himself crucified Jesus.

We have seen this already in a previous chapter. Those who were behind the crucifixion reckoned that if Jesus truly was who he claimed to be then he would never be crucified! God himself would have stopped it. The same God who stepped in and kept Abraham from offering Isaac as a sacrifice would have certainly stepped in if this Jesus of Nazareth really was the Son of God. But, owing to his alleged blasphemy – Jesus' claiming to be God – the Jews felt they were God's very instruments to destroy this imposter, this blasphemer. The Law – that a blasphemer should be put to death (Leviticus 24:14–16) – was on their side. They had a scriptural mandate to crucify Jesus. They were merely upholding the Law. It was the clearest case of obedience to the Law that one could conceivably imagine. So did they have guilty consciences in having Jesus nailed to the cross? Not at all. It was, to them, the easiest judgment to call in Israelite history.

The official position of the ancient Jews was that *God* did it – he himself smote Jesus of Nazareth. The Jews were merely God's obedient servants.

To put it another way, despite Jesus' goodness – for nobody could find a fault in him – the Jews felt that there had to be something fundamentally wrong about Jesus. Mind you, they had no objectivity about themselves – they did not acknowledge that: 1) they were actually jealous of him; and 2) he did not fit their preconceived notions as to what the Messiah would be like. They were therefore determined to find something that was absolutely wrong about Jesus. An unmistakable flaw. It was their job to find it. Surprise, surprise: they found it! "The high priest tore his clothes and said, 'He has spoken blasphemy! Why do we need any more witnesses? Look, now you have heard the blasphemy. What do you think?' 'He is worthy of death,' they answered." (Matthew 26:65–66) This is because he had claimed to be the Christ, the Son of God, and then added: "But I say to all of you: In the future you will see the Son of Man sitting at the right hand of the Mighty One and coming on the clouds of heaven" (Matthew 26:64).

Their reasoning, then, was like this. Had Jesus been an innocent man, and had he upheld the Law as he claimed he would do (Matthew 5:17), God would have rewarded him. He would have been openly vindicated. It would have been clear to all the Pharisees, Sadducees, and priests that Jesus was God's Messiah. For how could the whole of the Jewish establishment have missed such a Messiah?

But, said Isaiah, "We esteemed him not." It was a deliberate choice not to esteem him. "And quite rightly too!" they all would have said – in other words, by not esteeming Jesus, they believed they were on the side of truth. Although they would have to admit that Jesus did some good, such as carrying our sicknesses (no Jew doubted that Jesus healed people), it was God who rendered the righteous verdict: Jesus was worthy of death. He was a marked man – that is, in God's eyes – all along. The ancient Jews were simply agreeing with God.

I have often wondered what those who were actually healed by Jesus thought when they heard Jesus was crucified. Think of those who were demon-possessed – and delivered. Consider the man at the pool of Bethesda who had been lame for thirty-eight years – then suddenly walked. What about the blind people who were healed? I think about the woman of Nain, whose child was raised from the dead by Jesus during the funeral procession. I wonder what she thought! The miracles were so vast, said John, that: "If every one of them were written down, I suppose that even the whole world would not have room for the books that would be written" (John 21:25). So picture this: one by one, countless thousands got word that the man who healed them – turning their lives around – had been sentenced to death by crucifixion because he was a blasphemer! What must they have thought? "Was I healed by an imposter?" "Did a man who blasphemed heal me?" "How could I have been healed?"

And yet it must be said that people not truly walking with the Lord *have* been used in changing lives. It is true. The gifts of God are irrevocable; "without repentance" (Romans 11:29, AV); therefore one who is not walking with the Lord could be used of the Lord nonetheless. There are countless people who have come to the Lord through the preaching of famous television evangelists who were simultaneously living double lives. So when people who were changed or healed by them hear of the evangelist's immorality they must have asked: "How could such people have changed me?" The answer is: because it is true! My old mentor, evangelist Rolfe Barnard (1904–69), used to say that God uses a crooked stick to draw a straight line!

However, not so with Jesus. Jesus was perfect and absolutely without sin (Hebrews 4:15; 1 Peter 2:22). Whereas a few healings and miracles in the last two thousand years might have been accomplished by phony and fallen men, what Jesus himself accomplished cannot be compared to these people. Jesus "took up our infirmities and carried our sorrows". He reached out to the fallen and took on their case; he identified with those who were rejected, those who were weak, those who were ill and demon-possessed. Thousands could have come forward to testify to what Jesus did for them. And the authorities knew this too.

But the authorities wanted Jesus out of the picture. He did not match up to their theological assumptions about the Messiah. So they had to find something for which they could justifiably accuse him. Jesus handed their wish to them on a silver platter: "You will see the Son of Man [meaning himself] sitting at the right hand of the Mighty One and coming on the clouds of heaven" (Matthew 26:64). This language was similar to the son of man from Daniel 7:13: "There before me was one like a son of man, coming with the clouds of heaven." That was enough; that did it. For the son of man from Daniel had come to be regarded in ancient Israel as a God-like figure. The charge of blasphemy overruled all the miracles, all the good Jesus did, all the sympathy he showed toward the hurting – not to mention his teaching.

Matthew applied Isaiah 53:4 to Jesus' miraculous works. Jesus healed Peter's mother-in-law, then drove out the spirits "with a word and healed all the sick". Matthew stated that "this was to fulfill what was spoken through the prophet Isaiah: 'He took up our infirmities and carried our diseases'" (Matthew 8:17). Since Jesus' carrying our infirmities and diseases was seen as taking them to the cross, this passage – along with Isaiah 55:5 – is sometimes used to show that healing is in the atonement of Jesus. I will deal with this in the following chapter.

The people in those days *used* Jesus, that is, they

took advantage of his healing powers. He could heal the sick and cast out demons – indeed, he could overcome evil spirits that were beyond the power of the disciples (who were otherwise having considerable success). The disciples admitted that "even the demons submit to us in your name" (Luke 10:17), but that they came across some cases too big for them. "I begged your disciples to drive [the evil spirit] out, but they could not," said a desperate father to Jesus. But this was no problem for Jesus. He healed the demon-possessed child and "they were all amazed at the greatness of God" (Luke 9:40–43).

My point is this: despite all the good Jesus did, his miracles went by the way when the religious authorities were determined to get rid of him. Once they were satisfied that Jesus was a blasphemer they could pass the buck to God himself. Isaiah saw it all coming: "We considered him stricken by God, smitten by him, afflicted."

The Authorized Version has this translation of Isaiah 53:4: "Surely he hath borne our griefs, and carried our sorrows." This shows the heart of Jesus toward those who are hurting. When Jesus perceived sorrow in Mary and Martha at the tomb of Lazarus, he "wept" – as we see in John 11:35, famous for being the shortest verse in the Bible. If one is looking for someone who will feel with you, weep with you, and not moralize, Jesus is that person. Even though Mary and Martha were angry with Jesus that he did not turn up in time to heal Lazarus – and though Jesus knew he would be healing Lazarus in a few moments, he wept with them. He felt what they were feeling. He carried their griefs even before he went to the cross. The word translated "infirmities" means sickness in Hebrew. He carried them on himself, taking away such griefs or sicknesses from the people. But when he took them it did not mean that he then began to grieve or get ill; instead, the maladies evaporated into thin air. It was as though he could say to griefs, sorrows, infirmities, and illnesses: "Come to me." They obeyed and disappeared.

When Jesus was on the cross they watched with further smugness. The chief priests and the teachers of the Law mocked him among themselves. " 'He saved others,' they said, 'but he can't save himself! Let this Christ, this King of Israel, come down now from the cross, that we may see and believe' " (Mark 15:31–32). As long as Jesus remained on the cross they felt vindicated. Had he been the Son of God he *would* have come down, they reasoned.

Was it the Jews – or Pilate?

As for those chief priests, they were powerless to crucify Jesus. They had to go through the authorities. They took Jesus to Pontius Pilate, the Roman governor. The Jews were under Roman rule. They lived in an occupied land. They hated Rome, they hated the Roman soldiers, and they hated Pilate. They lived for one thing – the Messiah, who would come and overthrow the Roman tyranny. However, they needed Pilate to approve of the capital punishment of the day – crucifixion. They did not have the legal right to crucify anybody. This was the sole prerogative of the Romans. So the Jewish authorities took Jesus to Pilate.

They told Pilate lies about Jesus. The whole assembly rose and accused Jesus with one untruth after another. They said that Jesus was "subverting our nation. He opposes payment of taxes to Caesar and claims to be Christ, a king". Pilate asked Jesus if he was the king of the Jews. "Yes." Pilate's response: "I find no basis for a charge against this man" (Luke 23:1–4). But the moment Pilate noted that Jesus was a Galilean, he sent him to Herod.

Was it Herod?

King Herod, whom the Jews also hated, happened to be in Jerusalem at the time. When Herod saw Jesus, "he was greatly pleased, because for a long time he had been wanting to see him. From what he had heard about him, he hoped to see him perform some miracle. He plied him with many questions, but Jesus gave him no answer" (Luke 23:6–9). When Jesus gave no answer, Herod became indignant. He and his soldiers ridiculed and mocked him. They dressed Jesus in an elegant robe, and sent him back to Pilate.

Herod had the power to stop the whole procedure. He chose not to stop it. You could therefore say that Herod too was responsible for Jesus' crucifixion. "That day Herod and Pilate became friends – before this they had been enemies" (Luke 23:12).

So was it Rome?

When Pilate saw Jesus a second time he called the chief priests, rulers and the people to say that he had examined Jesus and found "no basis for your charges against him. Neither has Herod, for he sent him back to us; as you can see, he has done nothing to deserve death. Therefore, I will punish him and then release him" (Luke 23:13–16). At that point, "with one voice they cried out, 'Away with this man! Release Barabbas to us!'" (Luke 23:18). Barabbas was a condemned criminal. There was a prevailing Passover custom that a criminal could be set free in the place of another condemned man. In other words, Pilate could commute the death sentence. The chief priests and people demanded that Jesus be executed in Barabbas' place. Pilate then asked the people: "Which one do you want me to release to you: Barabbas, or Jesus who is called Christ?" They answered: "Barabbas!" Pilate then asked the crowds: "What shall I do, then, with Jesus who is called Christ?" According to Matthew, they all answered, "Crucify him!" But Pilate asked: "Why? What crime has he committed?" They shouted all the louder: "Crucify him!" There is an ominous sentence in all this: "Their shouts prevailed" (Luke 23:23). How interesting. Their shouts prevailed.

What followed was that "Pilate decided to grant their demand. He released the man who had been thrown into prison for insurrection and murder, the one they asked for, and surrendered Jesus to their will" (Luke 23:25).

You can therefore make the legal case that it was Pilate alone who crucified Jesus. Whereas Herod could have stopped the procedure, Pilate was the one who ordered that Jesus be crucified. You can therefore say that Rome was responsible for Jesus' death.

If you want to be technical, you can lay the blame for Jesus' crucifixion on the Roman soldiers. They were the ones who physically crucified Jesus. I don't think a single Jew drove in a nail. The governor's soldiers took Jesus and crucified him (Matthew 27:27–31; Mark 15:16–20).

Or was it the Jews?

We now get closer to the painful issue that involves the Jews. It was Herod who could have stopped it. It was Pilate who ordered it. But he, although in a rather detached manner, tried to talk the Jews out of crucifying him. "Why? What crime has he committed?" he asked (Matthew 27:23). But, as we saw above, their shouts prevailed. Pilate could also see that an uproar was starting. He took water and washed his hands in front of the crowd. "'I am innocent of this man's blood,' he said. 'It is your responsibility!'" (Matthew 27:24).

We now approach the most sobering, melancholy and memorable lines in all Holy Writ. We might wish the Jews had not said it, but they did. "All the people answered, 'Let his blood be on us and on our children!' " (Matthew 27:25). If we take this account seriously – and I do – it is plain to me that the Jews were responsible for crucifying Jesus. Herod would not have ordered it. Pilate would not have ordered it. Jesus' crucifixion would never have taken place apart from the Jews' demand.

As to whether God himself took this seriously is a separate issue. Some interpreters refer to ancient Israel's response to Moses, drawing a connection. Israel responded publicly to the Covenant, "Everything the Lord has said we will do" (Exodus 24:3), a word which bound them and (some argue) their children as well. The question has therefore been raised: to what extent were the Jews' words binding for their offspring? Did God hold all Jews not yet born responsible forever? Or was that generation of Jews two thousand years ago solely responsible? Did they have authority to speak for their children? Because they said, "His blood be on us and our children," does that mean that successive generations were under a curse? Did God hold all Jews from that day forward responsible for Jesus' death?

It is this line in Matthew 27:25 that fertilized the soil for anti-Semitism in the church. The early church picked up on this verse and this line of thinking continued right to the day of Martin Luther who, I am ashamed to say, became very anti-Semitic. I am very sorry about this, since I love Luther's teaching of justification by faith alone. But I believe Luther was quite wrong to take this line. But he was not the first and, sadly, won't be the last.

My view is that the Jews were responsible for Jesus' death but there is no clear evidence that they had authority to pass a curse on to successive generations of Jews.

Although blindness came on Israel and God opened the door to Gentiles (Romans 11:7–12), the door has always been open to *all* people who would accept the Gospel. There have been countless Jews who have been converted. Never forget that Saul of Tarsus was a Jew. I also believe with all my heart that the blindness now on Israel is about to be lifted, and that it won't be merely dozens but hundreds of thousands (perhaps millions) of Jews who will be converted before the Second Coming of Jesus. I will only add that, in my opinion, those Jews who are converted should own the sin of that generation two thousand years ago and admit the truth about the Jews' responsibility. I think it is sheer folly to say the Jews were not responsible. They were, and all Jews who come to Christ should say so.

Did I do it?

But there is more. When the Holy Spirit lifts the blindness on *any* of us – for we are *all* blind until God steps in (2 Corinthians 4:4) – we begin to see who really crucified Jesus. I did. You did. We all did. He died for *our* sins – not his. He never – ever – sinned. He took our punishment, as we will see in more detail below. But what will emerge – it is only a matter of time – in each of us is that *we* crucified Jesus. Don't blame the Jews. Don't blame Herod. Don't blame Pilate. Don't blame the soldiers. We all sent him to the cross. Indeed, some of the greatest hymns in church history demonstrate this:

Was it for crimes that I had done, He groaned upon
the tree?

Amazing pity! Grace unknown! And love beyond
degree!

Isaac Watts (1674–1748)

In evil long I took delight unawed by shame or fear;
Till a new object struck my sight, and stopped my
wild career.
I saw one hanging on a tree in agonies and blood;
Who fixed his languid eyes on me as near his cross
I stood.
Sure never to my latest breath can I forget that look;
It seemed to charge me with His death though not a
word he spoke.
My conscience felt and owned the guilt and plunged
me in despair;
I saw my sins His blood had spilt and helped to nail
him there.

John Newton (1725–1807)

Who crucified Jesus? You and I did.

God did it

But there is more. The buck stops with the sole architect
of the crucifixion – God himself. It was God's idea from the
beginning of creation. God chose Jesus "before the creation

of the world" (1 Peter 1:20). Again and again, especially in the fourth Gospel, Jesus is seen as "sent". Jesus was the Word that was made flesh. "In the beginning was the Word, and the Word was with God, and the Word was God… The Word was made flesh and made his dwelling among us" (John 1:1, 14). He was thus "sent" into the world (John 3:17). " 'My food,' said Jesus, 'is to do the will of him who sent me and to finish his work' " (John 4:34). That "work" was to die on a cross for the sins of the world.

Jesus went to the cross in the sovereign, predetermined will of God. God used "the help of wicked men", said Peter (Acts 2:23). This meant Herod, Pilate, the Jews, and the soldiers. The entire scenario was evil. Jesus did not get a fair trial. He had done nothing worthy of death, as Pilate concluded. Yet Pilate cowardly submitted to the wish of the Jews. But never forget Peter's words on the Day of Pentecost: "This man [Jesus] was handed over to you [the Jews] by *God's set purpose and foreknowledge*; and you [the Jews], with the help of wicked men [Herod, Pilate, the soldiers], put him to death by nailing him to the cross" (Acts 2:23). It was central to the theology of the earliest church that God was ultimately responsible for Jesus' dying on a cross. It was absolutely, irrevocably and unmistakably predestined. The prayer that ended with the place being shaken included these words: "They [Herod and Pilate, the Gentiles and the people of Israel] did what *your power and will had decided beforehand should happen*" (Acts 4:28). God himself was behind it all.

Who crucified Jesus? The bottom line – as we will see again and again below: God himself did it. They said: "We considered him stricken of God." The irony is, they were right.

CHAPTER FIVE

Jesus Punished – Why?

But he was pierced for our transgressions,
he was crushed for our iniquities; the
punishment that brought us peace was upon
him, and by his wounds we are healed.

ISAIAH 53:5

We are now getting to the heart of the Gospel: that Jesus took the punishment that you and I deserve. This is perhaps stated even more clearly in Isaiah 53:6 – "the Lord has laid on him the iniquity of us all" – which I will deal with in the following chapter. For the iniquity put on Jesus is what happened when Jesus was on the cross.

This is an amazing teaching! There is none like it anywhere else in the world. All other religions – all of them (no exceptions) – teach that Heaven (or whatever name you call it) is what we get as a result of our good works. The idea is that we get to Heaven by what we do for God. There are many people who call themselves Christians who actually believe that too. They think that they get to Heaven by what they do. And they are so wrong. They are deceived. They are not truly Christians. And so are you not a Christian if you have thought that you get to Heaven by being a good person.

What Isaiah was able to see seven hundred years in advance, through the power of the Holy Spirit, was: 1) what the Messiah would be like; 2) what he would do for us; and 3) why. This is the reason Isaiah 53 has been so important throughout the history of the Christian church, beginning with Matthew and continuing in the book of Acts. Isaiah was written so clearly that it is amazing that anybody, especially a Jew, could read this chapter and not see the obvious. But obvious though it is to me – and, I hope, to you – only the Holy Spirit can make it plain.

Some readers may know that I used to be a door-to-door vacuum cleaner salesman. Many years ago I sold fancy and expensive vacuum cleaners in South Florida – mostly in Fort Lauderdale and Miami. One of my customers was Nathan Darsky, the founder of the American Beverage Corporation. He was a Russian Jew who came to America early in the twentieth century, and did well for himself. I was proud to have sold him a vacuum cleaner. But a surprising friendship emerged. He liked me for some reason, possibly because I asked to pray for him. He wanted me to come and visit him – often. I did. I remember taking Rolfe Barnard, to whom I referred in the previous chapter, to meet Mr Darsky. I invited Mr Darsky to have a meal with Louise and me in

Fort Lauderdale. He accepted, and I spent that day praying for him. My chief desire was to lead him to Jesus Christ. He arrived on time in his chauffer-driven car, and brought a gift for our son T. R. who was barely a year old. We prepared the best meal we could come up with. After the meal I began to read the Bible to him. He did not seem to mind. I focused on Isaiah 53; I was so confident that he would see what was clear to me. But he didn't. All he could think of as I read the chapter – and he read it too – was (in his words) "the suffering of my people the Jews". He could not get past this. I tried other Old Testament passages as well, including Psalm 51. What the psalmist calls the Holy Spirit (verse 11), Mr Darsky interpreted to mean David's mind; his plea that God would not take the Holy Spirit from him, he interpreted as David's plea that he would not lose his sanity. He had his own interpretation of every single verse I mentioned.

My point is this. Only the Holy Spirit can make Old Testament passages clear. Once you see the true meaning you are amazed you had not seen it before. But only the Holy Spirit can make this clear.

If I may give another illustration, I used to fish in the Florida Keys. I became acquainted with a wily, wiry, silver fish called a bonefish that swims entirely in tropical waters. I had read articles about the bonefish, and how difficult they are to catch. These fish are very bony, and although one can eat them, most fishermen catch them for the sport and then throw them back into the water. The main thing is, they are extremely difficult to catch – a major challenge. It is virtually impossible to catch one without having someone to show you how to do it. But because I had read some articles on bonefishing I fancied that I could do it all by myself.

One day I went to a fishing camp called Gilberts, on Jewfish Creek near Key Largo, Florida. I said to the manager that I wanted to rent a boat to go bonefishing. He said: "Who is your guide?" I said: "I don't need a guide." He asked: "Are you a bonefisherman?" My reply: "Will be after today!" "Have you ever been bonefishing before?" "No." He looked at me kindly but firmly and said: "Nobody – nobody – goes bonefishing without a guide. You need somebody to pole the boat (like punting), you need a guide to show you the fish and to help you catch one." I said: "I don't need a guide. Will you rent me a boat?" "Yes, I'll rent you a boat." "Will you give me a map and show me where to go?" He did. I headed for Largo Sound in that little boat and looked for bonefish all day long. I came in several hours later. "How many did you catch?" the manager asked. "I didn't see any," I had to reply. There was a man listening to us who said: "I saw you over there – there were fish all around you." He himself had caught a huge bonefish that day in the same area I had looked for them.

Bonefishing requires hunting and fishing. A guide takes you to where the fish are and points them out. Although you are in crystal clear water only inches deep it takes an experienced eye to see them. And if they see you before you see them they take off like a torpedo. It requires a good eye, patience, and a lot of skill. I did not want to pay the price of a guide and I did not want to admit I needed one. I can tell you, I went back week after week, month after month – and never saw my first bonefish. I was too proud to admit I needed a guide and I did not want to fork out the money for one.

But after several months I gave in and booked a guide – one of the best (I was told). And where do you suppose he took me? Straight to Largo Sound where I had fished dozens of times without seeing any. The fish were there all the time, right before my eyes, but I could not see them. Within a minute or two of being with the guide he whispered: "Look! Eighty feet at ten o'clock [the stern being twelve], big bonefish – huge." But I could not see him – and so I missed him; the fish flashed away. Seconds later: "Look again! This time at one o'clock, there's another." I could not see a thing. However, later on the guide patiently prepared me. "There are fish coming. Keep your eye on that white spot at two o'clock. There they are!" I saw bonefish for the first time! I did not even know what they looked like in water until then! By the end of the day I hooked five bonefish. I will never forget it. What made the difference? I had to have a guide! The fish were there all the time! But I needed a guide to point them out to me.

Jesus said of the Holy Spirit that when he comes he will "*guide* you into all truth" (John 16:13). Why does one need a guide? Because the Bible is not understood naturally; it is by the Spirit. "The man without the Spirit does not accept the things that come from the Spirit of God, for they are foolishness to him, and he cannot understand them, because they are spiritually discerned" (1 Corinthians 2:14). Why is it that an unconverted man cannot understand the Bible? He thinks it is foolishness. He says: "I can understand history, philosophy, architecture, psychology, mathematics – and I should certainly be able to understand the Bible." But he or she can't! Why? Because only the Holy Spirit – our guide – can show what is there: Messiah, salvation, sin, redemption.

So too with Isaiah 53. This chapter is impossible to grasp without the Holy Spirit, and yet *with* the Holy Spirit it is easy to see. I can only pray for you, the reader, to have the illumination of the Holy Spirit as you read these verses. I am doing my best to make them simple and clear. I am even trying to be your guide! But unless the Holy Spirit comes alongside as you read – and drives this home to you and into your heart – it will make no sense to you.

When Isaiah says that the Messiah was "pierced" for our transgressions it is as though he can see the Roman soldiers hammering in the nails seven hundred years in advance. Crucifixion worked generally as I will describe to you now. The Roman soldiers would take a condemned man, and have him lie on two slabs of wood that crossed each other. The prisoner would lie on his back with outstretched arms. The soldiers would take the nails and drive them into the criminal's hands and into his feet. They used a rope to tie his head to the wood. They dug a hole into the ground, lifted up the cross as it slid into the hole, and hoisted it up into the air with the man hanging on the cross. He was held there by the rope around his neck and the nails that pierced his hands and feet. He would hang on the cross until he died. This was the Roman way of punishing a man for his transgression.

But Isaiah said that the man to whom he is referring was pierced for "our" transgressions. Not *his*. Ours. "Our transgressions", our sins. He was "crushed" ("bruised", in the AV) for "our iniquities". Isn't it amazing that Isaiah saw this event hundreds of years before the time? Every single person crucified in ancient history was paying the price for his own crime – usually murder. But Jesus was without sin. It was for "our transgressions", says the prophet, "crushed for our iniquities". But that is not the way the Sanhedrin (the ruling council of the Jews) saw it; they were punishing Jesus for his own sin – namely, the sin of blasphemy. But Isaiah vindicated Jesus in advance – his death was for our sins.

Isaiah 53:5, then, is an explicit prophetic reference to the crucifixion of Jesus. The word "pierced" comes from a word that also means "tormented". The prophet was describing physical, bodily pain. The Hebrew word translated "crushed" means extreme suffering. The Roman method of execution was designed to bring about the maximum kind of suffering. Instead of getting the death over and done in the shortest period of time, crucifixion was concocted to prolong the death and heighten the suffering. Except in certain countries today, where a less than instant beheading takes place, most governments that allow the death penalty at least make it instantaneous.

Therefore for some reason God sent his Son into the world at the time when Rome occupied Israel and when the death penalty was the most inhumane, awful, hideous, and painful method of execution ever devised by man. So let me soberly ask you to think about this the next time you take the bread and wine at Holy Communion. Consider what Jesus went through. Not for anything he did, but for what we did. But equally remember that the communion cup symbolizes how we get to Heaven – through the blood he shed that satisfied God's justice.

There are therefore two ways to approach Good Friday: historical and theological. Historically, what Jesus did is called *crucifixion*. Theologically, it is called *atonement*. Some interpreters of Scripture emphasize the historical and neglect the theological. And some emphasize the theological and barely emphasize the injustice of the trial and the pain of Jesus' death. To be balanced one must emphasize both. If you ask which is the more important, I answer: the theological. This is because Jesus suffered for us to save us from God's eternal wrath. Atonement for sin is the purpose of the cross. But never let us forget what Jesus was put through in order to save us from our sins and the wrath of God.

It is hard to take in. I am not sure we want to take it in. We are talking about unspeakable, unthinkable, and horrible *pain*. And yet the theological aspect of the cross is, if anything, harder to grasp. "For us he was made sin, Oh, help me take it in, " as Graham Kendrick put it (Graham

Kendrick © 1989 Make Way Music. www.grahamkendrick.co.uk. Used with permission).

The pain Jesus suffered on Good Friday was in fact threefold: physical, mental, and spiritual. The physical pain is what his body felt. God gave to the eternal *Logos* a body. In eternity he saw this, as put in Hebrews 10:5: "a body you prepared for me". The Eternal Son agreed to having a body before the Word became flesh. This body was to be the flesh of the Eternal Son from the moment he entered the womb of the Virgin Mary. Mary gave birth to a human being who was fully man, fully God. As a man Jesus could suffer pain: hunger (Mark 11:12), thirst (John 19:28), tiredness (John 4:6), and the need for sleep (Mark 4:38). The same body felt the pain which began with the flogging (Matthew 27:26). It is thought Jesus was too weak to carry his cross, which is probably why Simon of Cyrene was forced to carry it for him. He was fully man.

Jesus' mental anguish began in Gethsemane as he anticipated the cross, sweating what appeared to be drops of blood (Luke 22:44). Consider the humiliation – being stripped of all his clothes. All those who were crucified in Roman times were naked. There stood near the cross his mother, his mother's sister, and his convert Mary Magdalene. Imagine too the hurt and shame Jesus experienced as he saw these three women having to watch. Jesus was not even allowed to say a word of encouragement to them. He might have wanted to say to Mary Magdalene: "Mary, it's OK – don't worry; I am suffering for the sins of the world, all is going according to plan." His pain was thus intensified by not being able to make these women feel better.

The greatest pain of all however was the anguish, as we have seen already, of having the Father apparently turn his back on Jesus. This is when he cried out: "My God, my God, why have you forsaken me?" (Matthew 27:46). He was being "crushed for our iniquities". Our iniquities, sins, and transgressions were *transferred* to Jesus as though he were the guilty one.

Jesus was punished for our sins. He who knew no sin was made sin for us (2 Corinthians 5:21). It was the "punishment that brought us peace". Jesus had done nothing to deserve punishment. But Isaiah uses the word "punishment" (or "chastisement" in the AV and ESV). Why? The answer is: *sin had to be punished*. Had the sins of the world not been transferred to Jesus, then *we* (you and I) would be punished. But Jesus was punished for us. He took the punishment we deserve. In a word: God punished Jesus instead of us. Therefore all who transfer their trust in their good works to Jesus' death will be spared the wrath to come. But it is required that we trust what Jesus did. As John Calvin put it, all that Jesus did and suffered for the world is of no value until we believe.

Isaiah tells us that this punishment "brought us peace". This is huge: "since we have been justified through faith, we have *peace with God*" (Romans 5:1). Peace means calmness or rest – the opposite of war. In both Hebrew and Greek the word for peace refers to a *state* – like "time of peace" or "state of peace". It does not refer primarily to a relationship between people or even an attitude, but a state. Before Jesus died the whole world was in a state of war, God being the enemy. But Jesus changed that by being punished for us. This means our state of war with God has been reversed: we now have a state of peace. Until Jesus shed his blood, then, you and I were in a state of war with an omnipotent, just, holy, wrathful God. We were God's enemies because of our sins. But when Jesus died that state was reversed: we now have peace with God.

It is the best state you can find on this planet! You may want to have a different relationship with certain people. But the most important relationship you have – or ever will have – to reckon with is your state, or standing, before God. He is the one person you surely do not want to have as an enemy. Ever. The way to make friends with God is not by your promise to do better or by trying to butter him up by saying nice things, or to impress him by your good deeds (which annoys him). The only way to make peace with God is to appeal to the blood of his Son. That blood is the most precious commodity in the history of the human race. Jesus' punishment is what makes for peace. And Isaiah saw precisely this seven hundred years before it happened!

And yet when you see this you *feel* peace! Knowing that God is appeased makes you feel *so* good inside. It is wonderful. It means you will not go to Hell. It means you have been forgiven of your sins. It means you have escaped the eternal wrath of God. Another way of putting it is this:

when you have peace *with* God (that comes from faith in Jesus' blood) you are given the peace *of* or *from* God. It is the witness of the Holy Spirit – peace.

Isaiah added another beautiful phrase: "by his wounds we are healed"; "by his stripes we are healed" (Isaiah 53:5 AV, ESV). The wounds or stripes refer to the open gashes on his body from the flogging, but also the wounds from the crown of thorns and the nails. These wounds give us healing. His stripes did not heal him – he went on to die. But they heal us. They give us peace. Peter quotes this phrase: "By his wounds you have been healed" (1 Peter 2:24).

Is healing in the atonement?

We saw in Isaiah 53:4 that he "took up our infirmities and carried our sorrows". We saw that "infirmities" means sicknesses or illnesses. When Isaiah 53:4 is quoted in the New Testament it is translated: "He took up our infirmities and carried our diseases." This was in the context of Jesus having healed Peter's mother-in-law plus people being delivered from demon possession and sicknesses. When Matthew says that Jesus healed "all the sick" he followed it with these words: "This was to fulfill what was spoken through the prophet Isaiah: 'He took up our infirmities and carried our diseases'" (Matthew 8:16–17). It is obvious, therefore, that when Jesus died on the cross he carried, or bore, our illnesses and diseases. Moreover, since Matthew quotes Isaiah 53:4 in connection with physical healing, the conclusion might be that we not only have forgiveness of sins in the atonement but even deliverance from the demonic and the healing of the body as well.

Not only that; Isaiah goes on to say: "By his wounds we are healed." However, Peter does not apply Isaiah 53:5 to the healing of the body. The context of 1 Peter 2:24 suggests that the healing he means is with reference to our spiritual relationship with God. It refers to healing of one's spirit or soul; it here means healing from having wandered like sheep going astray (1 Peter 2:25). This would have been Peter's opportunity to bring in healing of the body, but he didn't. This does not mean that Isaiah 53:5 does not mean healing of the body; I am only pointing out that Peter's use of it points to one's spiritual relationship with God.

A stronger case I believe can be made from Isaiah 53:4 – that Jesus carried our sicknesses and diseases – since Matthew clearly applied this to Jesus' healing people's bodies (as well as delivering them from evil spirits). I therefore believe we have grounds for appealing to Jesus' death on the cross for the healing of sickness, disease, and deliverance from the demonic. But I do not believe this is the primary reason Jesus died on the cross. I fear that some people have appealed to the atonement for physical healing far more than they have for people to be justified by faith. This diversion from the primary purpose of Jesus' atonement could amount to a complete change of emphasis and, if we are not careful, will allow people to forget the burden of Isaiah all along.

I have two objections to the view that healing is in the atonement in the sense that one can appeal to Jesus' blood for their healing with the same authority that they do salvation. First, it puts pressure on the person who is unwell – to be sure that he or she has enough faith. If, therefore, the person is not healed one often hears the reason: "You did not have enough faith." This leads to the poor person feeling guilty – and sometimes to despair. Jesus never condemned the sick person's lack of faith – ever. After all, only God can give faith (Ephesians 2:8). Secondly, we all have to die sometime! Those who appeal to healing in the atonement have to answer the question: when is it right for the person to go on to Heaven? This emphasis that everybody should be healed in my opinion makes for a lopsided, misguided, and theologically unsound view of the atonement. But there is more; I fear that those who stress healing in the atonement – that everybody can and should be healed – have little or no place for the sovereignty of God. We must never forget that God said to Moses: "I will have mercy on whom I will have mercy" (Exodus 33:19; cf. Romans 9:15). Like it or not, this shows that God may or may not always do what we ask him to do. The buck stops with him. He decides.

Scholar and teacher Dr Michael Eaton points out that "everything is in the atonement", that Jesus indeed died for *everything* – "the reconciliation of all things – resurrection body, new heavens and new earth". The mistake some make, he says, is presuming a false deduction: "Therefore I can switch it [healing] on and claim it now." Matthew 8:17 and

Isaiah 53:4 show that every aspect of redemption is paid for by the blood of Christ. But it "does not mean we can switch on 'Second Coming blessings' at will". Dr Eaton thinks that such people are: 1) "over-realizing their eschatology"; 2) neglecting the fact that we are *waiting* for the physical side of salvation (as in Romans 8:23) in a way that is "not true of the more spiritual side of salvation"; and 3) not seeing that healing miracles – when they come – are "flashes of glory", as in John 11:1–44. Such miracles are graciously given in the sovereignty of God! Michael reckons "maybe one day they will be more common, but it won't come by our 'switching them on' ". I totally agree.

My view therefore is that it is fair to *pray* for people's healing on the basis of Isaiah 53:4–5 and Matthew 8:17. But I believe it is wrong to make this the primary and major emphasis of one's ministry. If people are healed we have the atonement of Jesus to thank for it, but not all who look to the cross for healing are healed. Experience and Scripture show this. However, *all who look to the cross for salvation are saved*. And if one considers healing of the body and the saving of the soul to be equal privileges in Christ's atonement he or she is making a big mistake – and diverts people from seeing the main reason Jesus died.

What has happened in some places, sadly, is this. People are by nature often going to be more interested in healing here on earth than they are about going to Heaven. That said, however, if healing softens hearts toward the Gospel, I say: go for it! God may in these last days – both in the Third

World and in the West – use signs, wonders, and miracles to get people's attention. I am all for this. What worries me is that some who emphasize healing too often have little or no understanding of the sovereignty of God or the Gospel! That worries me a lot. They often overlook the book of Romans and especially Romans 4.

But if one is indeed true to the Gospel, and also prays for people's healing on the basis of Isaiah 53:4–5, I am thrilled. Just remember: not all are *healed* who appeal to the cross, but all are *saved* who appeal to the cross. Why? The main reason Jesus died is to take the punishment for our sins. To quote an old slogan: the main thing is to keep the main thing the main thing. The main thing: the Gospel. That is why Jesus died.

CHAPTER SIX

The Bible in a Nutshell

We all, like sheep, have gone astray, each of
us has turned to his own way; and the Lord
has laid on him the iniquity of us all.

ISAIAH 53:6

Martin Luther (1483–1547) has been quoted many times for calling John 3:16 "the Bible in a nutshell". But Isaiah 53:6 is the nearest equivalent to John 3:16 in the Old Testament. John 3:16 says that God so loved the world that he gave his one and only Son, that whoever believes in him shall not perish but have eternal life. Isaiah 53:6 basically shows two things: that we are all sinners but God has shown his love by transferring the guilt of our sins to Jesus who has paid our debt.

The whole of the Bible can be summed up as: the state of fallen humankind and the love of God. To put it another way, man's natural response to God's love is that we all, like sheep, have gone astray and lived lives according to our own wicked ways but God has shown mercy by putting our sins on Jesus.

Our being like sheep and going astray is our ungrateful response to God. But how can such wandering be a response to God? It is because God has revealed himself by creation and through our consciences. Creation is proof of God's existence. Indeed, "the heavens declare the glory of God; the skies proclaim the work of his hands" (Psalm 19:1). According to Paul, the wrath of God is revealed from Heaven against all godlessness and wickedness of men who "suppress the truth by their wickedness". Yes, "what may be known about God is plain to them, because God has made it plain to them. For since the creation of the world God's invisible qualities – his eternal power and divine nature – have been clearly seen, being understood from what has been made, so that men are without excuse" (Romans 1:18–20). What Paul is saying is that we responded to God's glory in creation by rejecting him. We have chosen to stray. We have chosen to walk in our own willful ways. We knew better. We are also without excuse. And yet Isaiah says that "we all, like sheep, have gone astray".

Let me tell you one thing you can expect on Judgment Day. When all men and women stand before God and hear their sentence of doom, it will come within the context of all hearts being revealed. We will see *exactly* what all people – rich and famous, rich or poor, educated and uneducated – were thinking. I think for example of the high profile atheists of our day, like those at Oxford or Cambridge. They put erudite and seemingly irrefutable arguments to justify their premise that there is no God. They are unafraid to speak as they do – apparently. And it would seem they have adopted their arguments with sincerity and great conviction. But what they are not telling you is what has been in their hearts for a long time and which they have suppressed: that God *has* been revealed to them and that they chose to reject natural revelation.

Any person who examines the heavens, astronomy, or the glory of this earth with all its beauty and grandeur – and who is totally and transparently honest – knows in his or her heart that there must be a Creator God behind this. All one need do is to examine the human body – the brain, the eye, or one's entire nervous system. Only an infinitely wise God could create these things. These brilliant scientists and physicists, says Paul, *know* these things. They will not admit to this now. But they will then – before all. They will admit to what they suppressed.

It is not unlike what was going on in the mind of Saul of Tarsus. Here he was determined to kill Christians. There was no hint that he was having private thoughts that he might be wrong. He engineered the martyrdom of Stephen, and was obsessed in his desire to get Christians to blaspheme. But the Lord Jesus Christ said to him: "It is hard for you to kick against the goads" (Acts 26:14). Only God knew what was really in Saul's heart. No one else did. Nor would he have admitted it to anybody had not God converted him.

So with those who deny the truth of God's existence

by creation: they all have consciences. There is, said Blaise Pascal (1623–62), a "gaping chasm" in every person that can only be filled by God. This must be addressed when we talk to those who do not know the Lord. In our Pilot Light ministry I learned always to speak to people's hearts, not their minds. As St Augustine (354–430) put it: "Thou hast made us for thyself; our hearts are restless until they find their repose in thee." You and I must keep this in mind when we talk to them. We have "inside information" regarding what is going on inside them, even if they deny this. Their consciences – and innate sense of right and wrong – testify to one's actions. But, says Isaiah, "all we like sheep have gone astray, each of us have turned to his own way". We have done this deliberately, knowing better; but that is our choice. It is called sin.

St Augustine also stated that there are basically four stages of man: 1) *posse peccare* (able to sin – the way man was created before the Fall); 2) *non posse non peccare* (not able not to sin – after the Fall of man in the Garden of Eden – called original sin); 3) *posse non peccare* (able not to sin – through the Holy Spirit's power after regeneration); 4) *non posse peccare* (unable to sin – glorification in Heaven). We are all born unable not to sin. This is why Isaiah could say: "All we, like sheep, have gone astray, each of us has turned to his own way." There are no exceptions. We are born with the propensity to sin. And yet we choose to sin. The wandering like a sheep is what we all choose to do. Yes, we are indeed born into sin by birth (Psalm 51:5) – not able not to sin. This is why it is easier to do the wrong thing than the right thing. You don't need to teach a child how to lie. We all come from our mother's womb speaking lies. "Even from birth the wicked go astray; from the womb they are wayward and speak lies" (Psalm 58:3). And yet at the same time it is a choice. Sin is a condition but also a choice. That is what Isaiah is saying – we all without exception make the choice to go our own way.

This means we have all got off the rails. We have disobeyed God's word. We didn't listen. We have backslidden to some degree, wandering from the fold – the standard God has set for his people. We have all been rebellious – like Jonah. God told Jonah, "Go", but Jonah said "No" (Jonah 1:1ff). We are all Jonahs. My first book was on Jonah, and when I was asked, "Why did you choose Jonah to inaugurate your ministry at Westminster Chapel?" I answered: "I am Jonah." I completely identify with Jonah – both the one who rebelled (Jonah 1 and 2) and the Jonah who sulked when he was not vindicated (Jonah 2 and 3).

Speaking personally, I regard the words "all we, like sheep, have gone astray" as among the most tender, gracious, and moving words that are to be found anywhere in the Bible. There are in fact two verses that often bring me to tears: 1) "All we, like sheep, have gone astray"; and 2) "He knows how we are formed, he remembers that we are dust" (Psalm 103:14). These two verses, inspired by the Holy Spirit (never forget that), show that *God knows and sympathizes with our weaknesses*. Long before God gave us a High Priest who is in touch with our weaknesses we had a God who knows all about us and still cares for us. When I slip and come short of the glory of God – as I continue to do from time to time – I remember these two verses.

Our sin does not take God by surprise. Jesus told Peter that he would deny him three times – having just said: "But I have prayed for you" (Luke 22:31). Jesus loved Peter while knowing that in a few hours this same Peter would deny knowing Jesus. There were no grudges against Peter. Jesus saw right through Peter and saw what was coming but prayed for his restoration. Indeed, it may be forgotten that the well-known verse John 14:1 – "Let not your hearts be troubled" – immediately follows Jesus' word to Peter: "Before the cock crows, you will disown me three times!" (John 13:38). This is an important time to remember that there were no chapters or verses in the original language. Therefore Jesus is saying to Peter (and the disciples): "Before the rooster crows, you will disown me three times! Let not your hearts be troubled." What a merciful, compassionate God we have!

Characteristics of sheep

An old friend of mine, Douglas MacMillan (now in Heaven), was a shepherd in the Highlands of Scotland before he became a minister. I asked him to tell me some things about sheep. He knew them well. His first comment was: "The basic habit of a sheep is to wander; to go astray." That seems to be a part of their very nature. Second, they always think that the grass is greener on the other side of the fence. Third, they follow one another; it is called the "herding" instinct. They club together. So when a sheep wanders on its own, says Douglas, something is wrong. Fourth, they are stubborn; they always want their own way. Fifth, which according to Douglas is less known, a sheep always wants to get back into the area in which it was born. "I've known of a sheep to come through mountainous terrains thirty-five miles to find the place of its birth." Sixth, they are "stupid", he told me. You can't teach a sheep a trick. Even cattle don't need a shepherd or sheep dog, but sheep do. They will wander into a dangerous area or cliff – and get stuck. They can't take care of themselves. They wander or stray with no thought of what is coming next; they have no thought of the future. Finally, said Douglas, a sheep yearns for authority and guidance; it always needs and wants a shepherd.

According to Isaiah, we all are like sheep. And if you take Douglas MacMillan's words as authoritative, we all tend to think the grass is greener on the other side of the fence. This is what makes us covet what does not belong to us. We think the other person is better off; we want what he or she has. As to the "herding instinct", this is peer pressure – to go with the crowd, to do what "everybody is doing". And yet, if we are like that "lost sheep" Jesus talks about, how wonderful that our Master doesn't give up on us – he goes "after the lost sheep until he finds it" (Luke 15:4). God is like that with all of us; we have all been that lost sheep. "How precious to me are your thoughts, O God! How vast is the sum of them! Were I to count them, they would outnumber the grains of sand" (Psalm 139:17–18). We are all stubborn, wanting our own way. This is called selfishness. As a sheep wants to get back to the area in which it was born so we all regress to the way we were born – sinners with a propensity to sin and a choice to sin, doing what is wrong rather than the right. If Douglas is right, we are all "stupid" – unteachable by nature. I myself testify to doing things that were, simply, stupid. Embarrassing. I should have known better, and yet I did know better! I just have done stupid things. We get stuck and are helpless unless our Lord stoops to our weakness and bails us out. "Your rod and your staff, they comfort me" (Psalm 23:4). A shepherd sometimes takes the crook of his staff to rescue a sheep in trouble. The Lord has done this for me a thousand times. I thank God that there is a Chief Shepherd. When we yearn for his authority and control over our lives he is there! "For you were like sheep going astray, but now you have returned to the Shepherd and Overseer of your souls" (1 Peter 2:25). Jesus said: "My sheep listen to my voice; I know them, and they follow me. I give them eternal life, and they shall never perish; no one can snatch them out of my hand" (John 10:27–28).

Could it be that you are a backslider? Backsliding is a term that generally refers to the true Christian. It means to slip back after you started on your journey to follow the Lord. There are degrees of backsliding, say, on a scale from one to ten. But God is calling you home at this moment. Come home! Come home! Are you like that hymn, "I wandered far away from God, but now I'm coming home"?

What is the hope for those who have gone astray? Isaiah now gives what is arguably the quintessential statement on the atonement of Jesus Christ: "And the Lord laid on him the iniquity of us all." To approach this phrase is like trying to climb Mount Everest – or explore the Grand Canyon. It is the most profound statement made by the prophet Isaiah. He saw seven hundred years in advance that God would lay on a Messiah all our sins. Jesus is that Messiah.

Good Friday

This verse points to Good Friday. At some point between midday and three o'clock in the afternoon on that Day of Days, God charged Jesus of Nazareth with all the sins of the world. In other words, God imputed to Jesus *all our sins*. Whether this moment lasted for three hours or a few minutes, I do not know. But there was a moment when Jesus was legally charged with being the world's greatest sinner. That was when Jesus cried out: "My God, my God, why have you forsaken me?" The hint from this cry of Jesus is that sin is so horrible that God would not look at his Son during this moment. He apparently turned his back upon Jesus. Consider all the sins of every person who ever lived – those who were famous, infamous, unknown – and add them up (if one could), and remember that Jesus was now regarded as legally guilty of every person's sins. When I think of my own, that is enough to make me blush before the angels. That was enough for God to turn his back on Jesus. Just mine. Now add yours. Now compute every human being from creation to the end of the age – countless billions and billions. The sins of the whole world and of all ages were transferred to him as though he were guilty. "God made him who had no sin to be sin for us." He who never sinned – ever – was "made sin", says Paul (2 Corinthians 5:21, AV).

Isaiah 53:6 and 2 Corinthians 5:21 go together as if they were twins. The reason that you and I have righteousness imputed to us when we believe the Gospel (Romans 4:5) is because sin was first imputed to Jesus. To impute is a word that means to "charge with", "reckon", "credit", "consider", or "regard as". God charged Jesus with our iniquity. God reckoned Jesus as sin. He was considered, or regarded, as sin – but "for us"! The Lord God Almighty laid on Jesus our sins – all of them. God *transferred* them from us to his Son – then punished his Son for our sins as though he committed them. That is why Jesus died. God is responsible for Jesus' death. Don't blame Herod, Pilate, the Jews, or the Roman soldiers – or even the devil; the buck stops with God. He was at the bottom of it all.

This is the heart of the Gospel. To miss the meaning of this phrase – "the Lord laid on him the iniquity of us all" – is to misunderstand the reason God sent his Son into the world. This verse is however possibly the most offensive verse in the Bible. It is the verse that some may prefer to sweep under the carpet. One of the worst things I have heard is that Isaiah 53:6 describes "cosmic child abuse", that God has done a horrible thing by punishing Jesus. I reply: that is a horrible thing to say.

What God did was to make it possible for you and me: 1) to be forgiven; 2) to be declared righteous; 3) to enter into an intimate relationship with him; 4) to gain an inheritance in his kingdom; and 5) to go to Heaven when we die. All of which was carried out by the Levitical priesthood – by their sacrifices of animals and culminating on the Day of Atonement (Leviticus 16) – and was perfectly, finally, and forever fulfilled by Jesus' death on the cross. The high priest, by the symbolic gesture of his hands, transferred the sins of the people to the bleeding sacrifice on the altar. On Good Friday, God Almighty transferred the sins of us all to Jesus of Nazareth who died as a sacrificial lamb.

Charles Spurgeon used to say there are two words you need in your theological vocabulary: "substitution" and "satisfaction". There is no Gospel apart from these two concepts. Substitution refers to the fact that Jesus was our substitute. He took our place. We are the ones who sinned. But Jesus stepped in and substituted for us and said, as it were to the Father: "Blame me for their sins." God did just that. He blamed Jesus for our sins. He who knew no sin was made sin. He was a sin offering. The second word – satisfaction – means that God was satisfied by the blood Jesus shed on the cross. For this reason he is looking for nothing else from you and me – no works, no effort, no good deeds – to satisfy his justice. Only faith. He was utterly, totally and completely satisfied by Jesus' death on the cross.

> **I need no other argument, I need no other plea;**
> **It is enough that Jesus died and that He died for me.**
>
> LIDIE H. EDMUNDS (1851–1920)

And yet there are two more words that I should introduce to understand more fully Isaiah 53:6 – "expiation" and "propitiation". Expiation means atonement by Jesus' blood; propitiation means that his blood has turned away God's wrath. Expiation is what the blood does for us – washes away our sins. Propitiation is what the blood does for God the Father – satisfies his justice so that he is pacified by Jesus' death. These two words provide us with a sound theological understanding of why Jesus died. Some people (I fear) are only interested in what the blood of Jesus does for *us*. They are usually not too interested in what the blood does for God. We live in a "what's in it for me?" generation. Have you ever asked: "What's in it for God?" You should. You and I must never forget that God is a holy, just God. He has been sinned against. Sin must be punished. Jesus paid our debt by dying for us. But the blood he shed turned God's wrath away. This means we won't be eternally lost in Hell – that is, if we rely on Jesus' blood for our salvation.

Many years ago Billy Graham told a sweet story about when he was made to appear before a judge for speeding in North Carolina. When he saw the judge his heart leaped in him. "Oh good," he said to himself, "I know this judge.

He will let me off." The judged asked Billy Graham: "How do you plead?" "Guilty, your honour," said Billy. The judge then sentenced Billy Graham to pay a fine of $100. Billy's countenance fell, but he walked over to the cashier to pay his fine. But the judge got there first! The judge reached into his wallet, then paid Billy's fine for him. Justice was satisfied, the law was satisfied. And Billy was no doubt both satisfied and humbled. That is what Jesus did for us. He paid the penalty of our sins.

This means that our debt has been fully paid. It means that we will not go to Hell – that is, if we rely on his blood. If you are still relying on your good works, I'm sorry: you are disqualified from all that I am writing in this book. But when you are prepared to put "all your eggs in one basket" – namely, Jesus' death for your salvation – you are saved forever.

And yet let us look at this more deeply. Sins that were "laid" on Jesus were, as I said above, *transferred* to him. This means that *all* the guilt of *all* the sins we have committed were transferred to Jesus of Nazareth when he was hanging on the cross. This means God imputed Jesus with the guilt of our sins – as if he himself committed them. It equally means that God does not charge *us* with sin. Paul used David as an illustration. When God credits believers with righteousness it is "the same thing", says Paul, as God not imputing sin to them. "Blessed are they whose transgressions are forgiven, whose sins are covered. Blessed is the man whose sin the Lord will never count against him", or, as the Authorized

Version puts it: "Blessed is the man to whom the Lord will not impute sin" (Romans 4:8; Psalm 32:1–2). Consider this: although David was a man after God's own heart (1 Samuel 13:14; Acts 13:22), David sinned unthinkably heinously when he committed adultery with Bathsheba and then murdered her husband (2 Samuel 11). It doesn't get much worse than that. And yet God did not impute sin to David; that is, God did not charge David with the sin. Why? Because the Lord laid on Jesus his iniquity. You will say: "But David's sin took place a thousand years before Jesus died on the cross." Granted. But Jesus' death covered *all people of all ages*. The reason David could write as he did in Psalm 32 was because of what was coming down the road – a thousand years later – when God provided a Saviour. After all, Jesus was the lamb slain from the foundation of the world (1 Peter 1:20; Revelation 13:8). The marvel is that all our sins have been transferred to Jesus. He is the one who was found guilty.

Iniquity

There is another important point to be made. What is "iniquity"? "The Lord laid on him [Jesus] the iniquity of us all." This is a Hebrew word that covers the *worst* possible sin. In ancient Israel there were various classifications of sins. You may wish to say "sin is sin" and that's that. But not so in ancient Israel. There were basically two types of sin: intentional and unintentional. The offerings carried out by the Old Testament priests covered only "unintentional" sins (Numbers 15:22–29). Sin with a "high hand" or by one "who sins defiantly" – deliberate or intentional sin – was not covered (Numbers 15:30). Such people were to be put to death. Always. Therefore all sins that were covered by the sacrifices during the period of the Law were sins of weakness and ignorance (Hebrews 5:2, 9:7).

Think about that. Only sins of ignorance were covered by the sacrificial system. This gave someone like David no hope – none whatever. But Isaiah used a word that covers what is *perverse* or *immoral*. The Law did not cover willful, deliberate sins – called sin with a high hand. But when David committed adultery and pleaded for mercy, he asked: "Blot out all my iniquity" (Psalm 51:9). Although living during the era of the Law, David was enabled by the Holy Spirit to plead for mercy regarding his gross sin. God sees the end from the beginning. The Spirit foresaw what Jesus' atonement would do and enabled David to plead for mercy. David could therefore know that the worst possible sin would be covered by God's ultimate sacrifice for sin. How does that make you feel?

When God transferred our sins from us to Jesus it meant that a *transaction* took place. God did business with all humankind on Good Friday. "God was reconciling the world to himself in Christ, not counting men's sins against them" (2 Corinthians 5:19). Until then God and man were "natural enemies", to use Jonathan Edwards' phrase. But because Jesus bore the punishment of our sins you and I can approach God with boldness, knowing we are fully accepted. It is all because of the work of a substitute who provided satisfaction to the Most Holy God.

God did business with the world on Good Friday; Jesus was the mediator. As the God-man he was able to satisfy both sides – God and man. God got satisfaction; man had a substitute in his place. The result: the greatest transaction that ever took place occurred on Good Friday – and when we transfer our trust to Jesus. Therefore this word "transference" is used two ways: God transfers our sins to Jesus; we transfer our trust (in good works) to Jesus. That is when the transaction results in our eternal salvation.

Tis done! The great transaction's done!
I am my Lord's and He is mine;
He drew me, and I followed on,
Charmed to confess the voice divine.

PHILIP DODDRIDGE (1702–51)

Although the iniquity of "us all" is put on Jesus, all he did is of no value until we believe. This is crucial. Salvation is a gift (Romans 6:23). But a gift is not ours until we accept it. I used to say to people: "You may know that the train at Victoria station on Gate 6 is going to Brighton, but it won't take you to Brighton until you get on it." Or, to put it another way, many years ago a man in Pennsylvania was sentenced to die in the electric chair. But at the last moment he was given a pardon by the governor. However, strange as it may seem, this man did not accept the pardon, and asked to die.

The case went to the Supreme Court. The verdict: a pardon is not a pardon until it is received; the man must die. He did. In much the same way, then, although Jesus has provided a full pardon for us by his death, it is not ours until we receive it. But when we receive this forgiveness it means that the transaction is final, complete, and eternal.

This transaction results in transformation. Those who discover that God no longer holds them guilty for their sins are transformed. We are not the same. "If anyone is in Christ, he is a new creation; the old has gone, the new has come!" (2 Corinthians 5:17). For one thing, the weight of our sins is lifted from us. The heaviness that comes from shame plus the fear of spending eternity without God is lifted from us. There is no guilt, there is no fear. The further consequence is that we have a life of obedience to the God who redeemed us. "Therefore, I urge you, brothers, in view of God's mercy, to offer your bodies as living sacrifices, holy and pleasing to God – this is your spiritual act of worship" (Romans 12:1).

And what if we are not obedient? I answer: God found out David and he will find out you and me. Although the guilt of our sin has been transferred to Jesus, the responsibility for showing gratitude by a holy life is very real. God puts us on our honour to live lives that glorify him. If we displease him we are subject to his disciplining, or chastening. "The Lord disciplines those he loves, and he punishes everyone he accepts as a son" (Hebrews 12:6). This chastening is not God "getting even"; he got even at the cross. "As far as the east is from the west, so far has he removed our transgressions from us" (Psalm 103:12). These words were penned by David who gave us Psalm 32:5 – and who knew the Lord's chastening perhaps more than anybody!

So don't be a fool. Just because our sins have been transferred to Jesus does not give you and me license to live irresponsible lives. We are bought with a price. "Therefore honour God with your body" (1 Corinthians 6:20). We are called to sanctification (1 Thessalonians 4:3). The doctrine of sanctification is the doctrine of gratitude. We can never thank God enough for our salvation. We are not saved by our sanctification; we are not saved by our gratitude. But the evidence that the transaction has taken place in our lives will be lives of devotion and thankfulness.

> Were the whole realm of nature mine,
> That were an offering far too small;
> Love so amazing, so divine,
> Demands my soul, my life, my all.

> ISAAC WATTS (1674–1748)

CHAPTER SEVEN

How Jesus Handled Injustice

He was oppressed and afflicted, yet he did
not open his mouth; he was led like a lamb
to the slaughter, and as a sheep before her
shearers is silent, so he did not open his
mouth.

ISAIAH 53:7

We are all called to be more like Jesus. We are to have Jesus'
attitude (Philippians 2:5), and we are to "follow in his steps"
since he has left an example of how we are to cope with
suffering (1 Peter 2:21). I am reminded of a word Josif Tson
once said to me: "How far are you willing to go in your
commitment to follow Jesus?"

Jesus' example presents an extremely hard challenge to
us. We shall examine it in this chapter.

How did Jesus handle injustice? How do you handle

injustice? Does it measure up to the way Jesus dealt with it? Consider the unfair things that have happened to you. When you were lied about, mistreated, taken advantage of, or were passively involved in a situation that was riddled with evil. What was your reaction in those times?

Isaiah has already explained that Israel would miss their Messiah because he did not measure up to their expectations. He told us that he would be rejected, be smitten of God and bear our iniquity. What Isaiah now does is to enter more deeply into the Messiah's suffering. "He was oppressed and afflicted, yet he did not open his mouth." This refers mainly to how Jesus handled injustice to himself. We know how he felt about injustices in the world. For example, when he saw blind people (there is nothing fair about being blind), he healed them. When he saw people who were diseased, he healed them. When he saw people who were demon-possessed, he delivered them. When there was a freak of nature – such as a violent storm – he stopped it.

Never think that God takes lightly the injustices of this world: poverty, famine, earthquakes, typhoons, tornadoes, diseases, and suffering. God allowed sin, evil, and suffering to enter into the world he made. I don't know why – nobody knows why. I only know that God permitted it. This planet had a distinguished visitor two thousand years ago: God himself. Yes, God came to this earth himself in the person of Jesus. Jesus is the mirror of God. If you want to know how God feels, take a careful look at Jesus. He who saw Jesus saw the Father (John 14:9). All that Jesus did was to carry out God's will for him. Jesus said he did nothing by himself but only what he saw the Father do (John 5:19).

One day God will send Jesus a second time. I have to tell you, if you are on the wrong side of justice – that is, you are willfully involved in what is unjust, unfair, and wrong – it means you will be dealt with when Jesus comes again. Yes. You may initially say, "I am sure that God is going to put things right", but if you are involved in injustice you will be part of the way God will deal with sin and evil. If you are not – in this moment – covered by the blood of Jesus, it means you are abiding under his wrath. When his wrath is revealed – and it will be (Matthew 3:7) – I would not want to be in your shoes for anything in the world. You should fall to your knees right now. For the Second Coming of Jesus will not be a happy event for you. It will be then that Jesus will clear God's name; all injustices will be put right. In the meantime we have the person of Jesus Christ as God's hint to us how he actually feels about injustice in this world. How Jesus felt and acted is the way God feels.

So what about injustice to yourself? Let us say you have a physical problem. You have your financial problems. You are worried over having enough to go around in the light of your responsibilities. Or suppose someone has lied about you and put your reputation in jeopardy. Through the internet, anybody out there can say what they wish – and you are left to the judgment of what people conclude about you. Have you been falsely accused? Are you about to be sacked? Are you the victim of a gross plot of injustice? Have you been misunderstood but have no way of defending yourself? Or better still, suppose you *do* have a way of defending yourself; the question is: should you do it?

I can only say that there is nothing you have had to endure – or will ever have to endure – which Jesus himself did not personally face. But only a thousand times worse. Keep in mind: Jesus was God; his deity was veiled in human flesh. This meant that no hint of deity was allowed to surface. Had you been present when Jesus was on earth you would have seen a *man* who blended in with all that was around him. You would have never suspected that he had come from beyond, that he was the Word that was in the beginning with God for he was God (John 1:1).

Injustices Jesus endured

What were the injustices Jesus endured? First, he was "oppressed". This refers mainly to mental suffering. Jesus' mandate was partly to "release the oppressed" (Luke 4:18). Peter said that Jesus went around doing good and "healing all who were under the power of the devil" (Acts 10:38; "oppressed" in the ESV). The devil can be the cause of severe mental torture. There are two levels: oppression (when Satan attacks from outside – and causes a heaviness or depression) and possession (when the devil controls a person from within). Jesus can deliver a person from either condition. The psalmist said, "I have suffered your terrors and am in despair" (Psalm 88:15), which I take as a reference to oppression, or satanic attack. Dr Martyn Lloyd-Jones always said: "God never oppresses us." Oppression is from the devil.

Sometimes mental, emotional, or psychological sufferings can seem worse than any other kind. Take worry, for example: how to make ends meet. It is when you fear that you will be left wanting. It may mean having anxiety over where your next meal is coming from or where you will live. Jesus said: "Foxes have holes and birds of the air have nests, but the Son of Man has nowhere to lay his head" (Matthew 8:20). This statement partly means that Jesus had to adjust to a lifestyle without a permanent home – and lived by faith with regard to his food, shelter, and clothing. He therefore sympathizes with the homeless and those who live without knowing the comforts of this life.

But perhaps you have fears not necessarily related to financial needs. Maybe you are worried as to how your children will turn out. Or what will be the outcome of an exam you've just had – or have to face? Will I be accepted? Will I be invited? Will I meet the right person? Will I have a friend? Will I be lonely? Mother Theresa reckoned that the greatest problem in the world was loneliness. When Billy Graham preached for us at Westminster Chapel his unforgettable subject was on loneliness. Jesus went through Gethsemane alone and died on the cross alone. Part of his anxiety too, as we saw previously, was on the cross when he was not allowed by God to communicate with his mother or Mary Magdalene in order to make them feel better. Part of his suffering was that he could not feel better by making them feel better.

Perhaps you are governed by anxiety? Or you live in what seems to be a permanent state of depression? Anxiety and depression are common denominators of nearly all psychopathology. Perhaps you look for at least one other person who will understand you. You hope that a counsellor, pastor, psychologist or psychiatrist will be able to help? Here is one certain thing: Jesus was tried, tested and tempted at all areas – just like us, although without sin (Hebrews 4:15). The point is, he understands. He will not laugh, scold, or moralize you. He is touched with *feeling* and takes on your case. Why? He himself knew what it was to be "oppressed", and he has never forgotten what it was like – even though he is now at God's right hand. He remains moved with compassion towards us. What a wonderful Saviour!

Isaiah also says Jesus was "afflicted". The word affliction may refer to either physical or emotional suffering. It is a word that simply means *pain* – whether mental or pain in the body. Part of the reason for his suffering was precisely so he could sympathize with us – "that he might become a merciful and faithful high priest in service to God" (Hebrews 2:17). One of the hardest verses in the Bible to understand is this: "Although he was a son, he learned obedience from what he suffered" (Hebrews 5:8). His affliction, then, was for us.

Therefore we must never think that God does not understand pain. I have never been persuaded that God is impassable, that he is not subject to pain or does not feel pain. This to me is quite wrong and purports a God afar off who is unbothered by the sorrows of this world. This is not biblical teaching. What Jesus felt, God felt. When we get to Heaven, I predict, we will discover that God was not only the most maligned person in the universe but the one who suffered the most. In order to prove this God came to earth himself – became flesh and was "afflicted".

Some of God's children apparently suffer more than others. I have known some Christians who seem not to suffer at all. I have also known some believers who have suffered horribly most of their lives – either from poverty, mental torture, or a perpetually bleak outlook. I only know that such people, assuming they did not shake their fists defiantly at God, will know blessing and reward in Heaven beyond the rest of us.

The Apostle Paul testifies to a "thorn in the flesh" – an affliction that God used to keep him from being "conceited" (2 Corinthians 12:7; "exalted above measure" in the KJV; or "too elated" in the ESV). It was so awful that he asked God three times to remove it. God said "No, you can't cope with it Paul": "My grace is sufficient for you, for my power is made perfect in weakness" (2 Corinthians 12:9). We won't know until we get to Heaven what Paul's thorn was. I have written a book on it – *The Thorn in the Flesh* – and have suggestions as to how God may send a thorn to us whether it be a handicap, unhappy living conditions, emotional suffering, an unhappy marriage, a sexual vulnerability, or an unhappy job situation. Most of us have a "thorn" of some kind. It is an affliction, an extreme form of being chastened or disciplined (see Hebrews 12:6–11).

Jesus' reaction to suffering

Isaiah adds a third description: "yet he did not open his mouth". Although Jesus was oppressed and afflicted he did not complain. He did not say a word – whether to God or to people. No murmuring. No grumbling. No questioning.

This also means that Jesus did not try to vindicate himself. The greatest freedom is having nothing to prove, and Jesus enjoyed such personal security that he did not try to prove himself or impress anybody. He got his vindication from pleasing the Father (John 8:29). It is what Paul calls being "vindicated by the Spirit" (1 Timothy 3:16), an internal witness that God's approval of him was sufficient.

When I examine God's attitude to grumbling, I am sobered. I suspect that if you (if you have this problem) and I knew just how much God hates our murmuring and complaining, we would stop it! He hates it. In 1 Corinthians 10:8–10 Paul lumps together three sins as if they equally grieve him: sexual immorality, testing the Lord, and grumbling.

Jesus set the supreme example. In the face of oppression and affliction he "did not open his mouth". He did not protest to Herod, the chief priests, or Pilate that he was not given a fair trial. He did not say to his Father: "How could you let them do this to me?" He did not say to them: "You have no right to treat me like this!" He did not gather a following to campaign on his behalf. He did not lift a finger or say a word.

Isaiah described the crucifixion event at this stage in slightly more detail: "He was led like a lamb to the slaughter, and as a sheep before her shearers is silent, so he did not open his mouth." According to Douglas MacMillan, whom I quoted earlier, sheep don't like the smell of blood. They back off from it. Douglas said: "You have to drag a sheep to the slaughter house." Sheep, he said, are very stubborn and very difficult to drag. But he added: "Only a lamb that was hand-fed by his shepherd would follow his shepherd where other sheep have been killed. Such a lamb would trust his shepherd." Jesus voluntarily submitted to what was absolutely abhorrent to him – like a lamb to the slaughter – but he trusted his Father all the way to the cross.

Crucifixions were a common sight in Judea during Roman times. Jesus could see what they were like; he knew what the Romans would do to him. There was nothing attractive about the cross. And when it came to be his turn, a date in history toward which the whole of his life was moving, he submitted without a word.

Let us suppose that something terrible you have read about in newspapers, seen on television, or heard about in the office, was now happening to *you*. How would you cope? Can it be said of you that you did not open your mouth? As for Jesus, "When they hurled their insults at him, he did not retaliate; when he suffered, he made no threats. Instead, he entrusted himself to him who judges justly" (1 Peter 2:23).

Jesus was robbed of all dignity and self-esteem. "As a lamb before her shearers is silent, so he did not open his mouth." Have you ever seen a sheep right after it has been sheared? It actually looks "naked". Jesus was stripped of all clothing. What portraits of Jesus on the cross don't show you is that he was naked on the cross. Imagine the shame and humiliation. And yet he "scorned" the shame (Hebrews 12:2). There is an interpretation of this translation of the NIV which suggests that Jesus refused to let it bother him. But it must have bothered him. He was forced to do what was abhorrent.

There was nothing remotely fair about Jesus' trial – that is, if you could even call it a trial. Tempers flared, emotions took over, and the chief priests got what they wanted. Pilate and Herod passed Jesus back and forth. Herod was pleased at the thought of meeting Jesus, hoping that he would perform a miracle – like a magician pulling a rabbit out of a hat! But Jesus simply stared at him and did not open his mouth. This to me was one of Jesus' most brilliant moments. Imagine being questioned by a king and saying absolutely nothing! Herod plied him with many questions, "but Jesus gave him no answer" (Luke 23:9). Those guarding Jesus began mocking and beating him. They blindfolded him and demanded: "Prophesy! Who hit you?" (Luke 22:64). There was no reply. Jesus was led back to Pilate, who asked him: "Where do you come from?" but Jesus gave him no answer (John 19:9). Can you imagine the willpower, the self-discipline, and strength of character required to stand before King Herod and the Governor of Judea and *not say a word*? Amazing! But, as I said, the greatest freedom is having nothing to prove and Jesus had nothing to prove.

How did Jesus handle injustice?

Jesus faced injustice and suffering by a voluntary submission. All that Jesus endured was by his own will. It was a choice – an act of the will – voluntarily submitting to what was ordained for him. Whereas sheep had to be dragged to the slaughter house – against their will – Jesus submitted voluntarily. "My food is to do the will of him who sent me and to finish his work" (John 4:34). So when his moment of destiny arrived there were no complaints, no protests, no marches, not even a hint of indignation. He just submitted.

If you are in a trial – or have one coming down the road – remember Jesus. He submitted. You and I must submit too. Today I had dinner with my pastor in Hendersonville, Tennessee. Both his parents have Alzheimer's disease. To be honest, I too have a fear of getting Alzheimer's. My father died at the age of 93, having had Alzheimer's (or dementia) for eight years. His father also had it. I am now 75. My time could be coming too. Will I submit to this voluntarily – and without grumbling? I pray so.

Jesus submitted to the cross with a valiant silence. Douglas MacMillan also made the observation that sheep are not always dumb; they will bleat or cry in distress. "But when sheared, they never complain, even when the shears clip the skin and cause bleeding." Isaiah said: "As a sheep before her shearers is silent, so he did not open his mouth." Behind Jesus' magnificent display of faith and character was a principle the Father had laid down centuries before: "It is mine to avenge; I will repay" (Deuteronomy 32:35). Vengeance is God's prerogative. Jesus was not going to rob the Father of showing his anger in due time. I myself have learned this across fifty-five years of ministry: don't deprive God of what he does better than us. The moment we take vengeance into our hands, God backs off – and nothing happens. But if we will take our hands utterly off the situation, refusing to clear our name or to vindicate ourselves, God rolls up his sleeves and steps in. He does it brilliantly, by the way. Don't elbow in on God's territory.

What Jesus was doing by not opening his mouth was suffering vicariously. It was not for himself. It was for us. It was a voluntary obedience. "For just as through the disobedience of the one man [Adam] the many were made sinners, so also through the obedience of the one man [Jesus] the many will be made righteous" (Romans 5:19). Jesus lived a sinless life – vicariously. He died a violent, sacrificial, but obedient death – vicariously. His obedience was a vicarious obedience. His sinless life was performed twenty-four hours a day every day of his life in order that this righteousness might be transferred to you. Therefore it was not for his sins that Jesus died; he never sinned. It was for our sins. The

God-man was made sin for us that we might be made the righteousness of God in him (2 Corinthians 5:21).

In a word: he took your place – and mine

And had you thought that God doesn't care? As St Augustine put it, if you were the only person that lived God would have sent Jesus to die for you. You may feel mistreated and abused. You may feel passed by – watching others get ahead. It is a funny old world, as the former British Prime Minister Margaret Thatcher once said. Good things happen to bad people; bad things happen to good people. Jesus was good. He was oppressed and afflicted, yet he did not open his mouth. This was so you would go to Heaven one day.

But you and I must not remain silent. It is our duty and privilege to confess him. Openly. Show that you are not ashamed of him. Share with one other person that you have trusted Jesus who died; you have trusted his blood and his righteousness. Identify with a church where the Bible is preached and Christ is honoured. And live the rest of your days bringing honour and glory to him.

CHAPTER EIGHT

Not Allowed to Live

By oppression and judgment he was
taken away. And who can speak of his
descendants? For he was cut off from the
land of the living; for the transgression of my
people he was stricken.

ISAIAH 53:8

There are three questions which the prophet specifically
raised in Isaiah 53. The first is: "Who has believed our
message?" (verse 1). Isaiah showed us that he saw clearly
what Israel's Messiah would look like and what he would
do – and that the people to whom he was sent would reject
him. The prophet therefore knew from the start that Israel's
promised Messiah would be a rejected Messiah. The second
question he raised was: "To whom has the arm of the Lord
been revealed?" Isaiah also knew that the Holy Spirit would
open the eyes of some. A few, but not all, would believe,
namely, those who were effectually called (John 6:37, 44).

The Holy Spirit is the only explanation for any conversion – at any time in history.

The third question is right in the middle of Isaiah 53:8: "Who can speak of his descendants?" In this chapter we will examine this question. Why did Isaiah ask it? Why did he speak of the Messiah's "descendants"? What can be said about them? The prophet's next phrase, not exactly an answer to this question, is not a happy thought: "he was cut off from the land of the living". A melancholy mood therefore pervades this verse. You could call the verse a continuation of the theme of what is just and what is unjust.

The question is a cry of anguish. Isaiah wondered whether any of the Messiah's generation protested. The grossest possible injustice was perpetrated before people's eyes – and who worried about it? Where were his descendants at this time? Why did they not speak up? Was there no relative who could roll up their sleeves and go to Herod or Pilate and say: "This is not fair. You cannot do this. It is not right." Isaiah's question was a cry of anguish. After all, the Messiah had done nothing but good.

But he was cut off. He died before his time, as it were. He was only 33 years old. He was sentenced to death without justice. "Cut off from the land of the living." Do you know what it is to cry out when you observe injustice right before your eyes? Or do you sit still and say: "I don't want to be involved." There are countless stories of people who have watched people being mugged – even raped – but did nothing. It was the way Jeremiah felt in his cry: "Why do we sit still?" (Jeremiah 8:14, in the KJV). So in a similar way Isaiah cried out.

Think of people you knew of who died young. You might think of those with wonderful futures laid before them; they had such wonderful possibilities – but they were taken. Why? Some of God's greatest servants were taken when they were young. The saintly Scottish preacher Robert Murray M'Cheyne (1813–43) died at the age of 29. David Brainerd (1718–47), missionary to the American Indians in New York, died at the age of 29. The man who would have become Brainerd's father-in-law, Jonathan Edwards (1703–58), himself died at the age of 55. John Bradford (1510–55), burned at the stake during the reign of Mary Tudor, died for his faith at the age of 45. John Calvin (1509–64) was 55 when he died. Charles Spurgeon (1834–92) was 58. My own mother died at the age of 43.

It seems so unfair when a person dies young, whether they be a baby, a child, a teenager, or an adult.

Jesus of Nazareth, born of a virgin, began his public ministry at the age of 30. The hope of Israel centered on him. "We had hoped that he was the one who was going to redeem Israel," the two people on the road to Emmaus said when they reflected on the crucifixion of Jesus (Luke 24:21). At the age of 33 he was "cut off from the land of the living". Having never sinned, his "crime" was telling the truth! He was not allowed to live.

"Who shall declare his generation?" (KJV). "Who shall speak of his descendants?" (NIV). "And as for his generation, who considered that he was cut off out of the land of the living?" (ESV). When a genius dies, the sort of question frequently asked is: "Who will take his place and carry on his work?" A genius, like St Augustine (354–430), Thomas Aquinas (1225–1274), Leonardo Da Vinci (1452–1519), or Michelangelo (1475–1554), comes along an average of every hundred years. There had been no one like Moses for several hundred years.

Jesus, however, was more than a genius. He was unique in all history. There has been only one God-man in all history – past, present, or future. And yet, when he finally came along, he was "cut off in the land of the living".

Isaiah preceded his question with a statement: "By oppression and judgment he was taken away." This referred to Jesus' arrest in the Garden of Gethsemane (where he was handcuffed; Isaiah referred to the inability to use his arms). He was suddenly under the dominion of the Jewish authorities and then Pontius Pilate.

Many thought he could not die. How could a man who raised the dead die? How could the man who walked on water die? How could a man who fed five thousand with two loaves of bread and two fish die? Some expected an angel to deliver him, to stop the ruthless, inhumane travesty of justice. Islam teaches that Allah actually delivered Jesus from the cross. But the Bible teaches that God not only allowed Jesus to be cut off, but that he was behind the entire scenario. This means, therefore, that the prophet who would be like Moses would have a premature death. But would not the prophet like Moses be spared of such injustice?

But the next thing people saw was his crucifixion. He was cut off. What, therefore, would happen to Jesus' teachings? There were no video recordings, no CDs or DVDs. Who could speak of his descendants? He didn't even have any children. He never married. Had all the good this man had done come to nothing?

Suddenly, Jesus cried out: "My God, my God, why have you forsaken me?" (Matthew 27:46). He then bowed his head and said: "It is finished" (John 19:30). People looked at each other. They said: "He's dead. He's actually dead. We can't believe it. He has been cut off."

And yet the cry of anguish was equally a positive cry of affirmation. After all, it was a triumph! "For the transgression of my people he was stricken." Jesus was not only blamed for the transgressions of Israel, but he voluntarily took the blame! Indeed, this was why he came and died!

Do you therefore know why he was cut off? Here is the answer: Jesus' purpose in coming in the first place was not to overthrow Rome, to change external structures of government, or to return the glory of David or Solomon to Israel. It was not to cleanse from without, but to cleanse from within. The purpose of Jesus' coming was to cleanse the *hearts* of men and women. But such a possibility was not even on Israel's "radar screen".

Suppose there was a prime minister, president, or royal figure who could erase poverty or unemployment. Suppose such a leader could raise everybody's standard of living.

Suppose all your problems – health problems, financial problems, emotional problems, social relationship problems – were solved all at once, or that suddenly the air was made totally clean, the waters throughout the world pure and all the trees green again? So what! *We all are still going to die one day.* And it was precisely because of your death – and the fact that you have to answer to a just God – that Jesus came. That is why he was "cut off".

Have you ever been told this before? Does it surprise you? Jesus did not come to be the wisest politician, the greatest military figure, or even the best teacher. He came to be "cut off" in order to die for our sins. The crucifixion was no accident. It was by the predetermined counsel of God (Acts 2:23). The reason Isaiah could see this, seven hundred years in advance, is that God knows the future and Isaiah was able to see the future by the Holy Spirit.

Jesus of Nazareth accomplished more in his thirty-three years than any person who lived twice or three times that long! Indeed, no person in human history did what he did – no matter how long they lived. And yet Jesus accomplished the greatest deed in human history in such a short period of time. He fulfilled the Law on our behalf (keeping it for us – since he was our substitute), he lived for thirty-three years without ever sinning, he believed perfectly in his mission, he obeyed the Father to the hilt, and then he satisfied the justice and wrath of God by the shedding of his most precious blood. No person ever attempted to do this – before or since. The ancient prophet, living in 700 BC, saw this in advance and wrote it up so that we had it succinctly in the fifty-third chapter of the book of Isaiah.

What Jesus came to do, then, he did. This, however, was not cleansing the government by a new kind of politics but cleansing us from our sins. Consider your own heart: the envy, the grudges, the anger, the secret thoughts, the self-pity. Worst of all, think of the self-righteousness – that something in all of us that makes us think we are OK without Jesus Christ's life and death. Jesus said to the aforementioned two people on the road to Emmaus: "How foolish you are, and how slow of heart to believe all that the prophets have spoken! Did not the Christ have to suffer these things and then enter into his glory?" Then he gave them an exposition of the Law of Moses and the words of the prophets, and explained to them "what was said in all the Scriptures concerning himself" (Luke 24:25–27).

To put it another way: what Jesus did on the road to Emmaus with these two people was what I am attempting to do in this book! He expounded the prophets, says Luke. This would almost certainly refer to Isaiah, especially Isaiah 53! What Jesus did perfectly when he explained the Scriptures – their hearts were left burning (Luke 24:32) – I am doing feebly by comparison. I can only pray that the Holy Spirit who inspired Isaiah will come alongside you as you read this book!

Isaiah's cry was not merely a call of affirmation but a call *for* affirmation. It was a call for you and me to affirm the reason he was cut off. You and I cannot sit still. We must cast a vote, rendering our verdict on whether Jesus' death was a sad, accidental, unexplainable event or that his being "cut off from the land of the living" was on purpose. What then do you say? Do you see the Messiah as being the one who came not to overthrow Rome or change governments but to die for our sins?

I speak now to Jews – who, just maybe, will pick up this book and read it. You have an opportunity to do what is long overdue among your people. Do not follow the majority of your fellow Jews. May the Holy Spirit open your eyes as you read these lines. If he does, you need to affirm the real purpose of Jesus' coming into the world two thousand years ago, and confess him as *your* Messiah, *your* Redeemer and Saviour, and *your* Lord.

Do not be like those who say: "If I had been there I would have accepted him." The truth is, we all would have been like them but for our eyes being opened by the Holy Spirit. We would have joined those who said: "He saved others, but he can't save himself. If you are the Messiah, come down from the cross" (Mark 15:31–32).

Isaiah's question, "Who can speak of his descendants?" must be answered. The question is, will you? Will you speak of his descendants? You may ask: "How can I speak of his descendants?" The answer is: you show yourself to be one of them! If you confess him, you become one of the family! The moment you confess that Jesus of Nazareth is God's Messiah – but also God's Son – you will be a child of God and a brother or sister to Jesus! Yes, Jesus was the only "natural" son of God – he was the God-man. You and I have been "adopted" into the family (Ephesians 1:5). That makes Jesus our brother; we are his brothers and sisters. We are his descendants.

Although Jesus had no natural sons or daughters – he never married – he has countless spiritual children; indeed, he has a multitude that no one can count (Revelation 7:9). As was promised to Abraham, "As numerous as the stars in the sky and as the sand on the seashore" (Genesis 22:17). No family that ever lived can match the size of God's family! Who can speak of his descendants? You can. I can. We all can. It is our duty and yet our supreme privilege. How do you do it? You admit that you are a sinner, that your greatest need is not a better job, a better home, a better situation, a better government, or a better society, but that your greatest need is to be forgiven of all your sins. Your greatest need is to be ready to die. Your greatest responsibility is to know you will go to Heaven when you die. Jesus, God's Messiah, was "cut off" in order that you and I will go to Heaven one day.

No natural relative came forward to claim Jesus' body. But a member of the true family of God did. His name was Joseph of Arimathea, a "disciple of Jesus" (John 19:38). He had been a secret follower of Jesus for some three years. But when the crunch came, Joseph came out of hiding and declared himself by going openly to Pilate to claim the body of Jesus.

Jesus came to his "own, and his own people did not

receive him" (John 1:11, ESV). You can do what the ancient Jews did not do: own Jesus as your own. If you are Jewish, you can indeed do what they did not do. You can do what other Jews are not doing. You can do what countless Gentiles are not doing. You may have to do it when you are a part of a small minority. But one day the whole world will proclaim him as Lord. Yes. "Every knee will bow before me; every tongue will confess to God" (Romans 14:11). But they won't be saved. Why? Because they will do it after Jesus openly reveals himself. Every eye shall see him (Revelation 1:7). Their bowing to him won't be done in *faith*; they will be doing it by command – to acknowledge God's Son before demons and angels. But they will not be saved. Only those who confess him now will be saved. Those who are descendants of God's Messiah must come out of hiding now, just as Joseph of Arimathea did. Will you?

Isaiah's cry of anguish and affirmation is also the prophet's confirmation of an incalculable accomplishment: "for the transgression of my people he was stricken". This is why Jesus was "cut off" and not allowed to die. This means that Jesus took the blame for Israel's transgression. Jesus died for our redemption. Isaiah is repeating what he said earlier: "the Lord has laid on him the iniquity of us all" (Isaiah 53:6).

There are two categories, speaking generally, of people who ever lived. First, there are those who accomplished virtually nothing good in their lifetime – and nothing by their death. Some left their mark on history – like Adolf

Hitler (1889–1945) or Joseph Stalin (1878–1953). But their accomplishments were almost entirely negative, resulting in the death and suffering of millions. But, second, there are those whose lives did great good – even though they were cut off at an early age. I mentioned certain people who died before they were 60. Robert Murray M'Cheyne's influence throughout the western world has been vast. Dr N. B. Magruder, the man who ordained me, regarded the biography and letters of M'Cheyne as being the most influential piece of literature in his own life. Jonathan Edwards published the *Life and Diary of David Brainerd* (John Wesley required that all his ministers read this book; there was a time that it was said that it was so inspiring and moving that it put more people on the mission field than any other body of literature except for the Bible). Edwards, the central figure in the Great Awakening in America (1725–50), was also the greatest theologian the American continent ever produced. As for John Calvin, to read western history apart from his influence would be like reading it with one eye shut. And as for Charles Spurgeon, his thousands of sermons are still in print today!

And as for Jesus? He was stricken for the transgression of his people – which in effect means that he died for his descendants. Indeed, it was because of Jesus' death that his descendants were as numerous as the stars and the grains of sand.

Jesus himself promised that the Holy Spirit would bring to people's remembrance what he taught (John 14:26).

We have the four Gospels (Matthew, Mark, Luke, and John) for a start. And yet the entire New Testament is all about Jesus. What a legacy! The calendar throughout the world is divided between BC (Before Christ) and AD (Anno Domini – the Year of our Lord). The entire western world has been shaped by the Christian faith. The Gospel penetrating Latin America, India, and China has resulted in millions of people being converted and has even raised the standard of living in parts of those countries by a considerable degree. Who can speak of his descendants? The world in a sense testifies to the difference the coming of Jesus Christ has made on civilization.

Jesus' life was "cut off". He was not allowed to live – for one reason: that you might live. He took your place, that you might go to Heaven one day and even have a better life in the here and now. God will even give you a little bit of Heaven to go to Heaven in.

CHAPTER NINE

Astonishing Prophecy Fulfilled

He was assigned a grave with the wicked,
and with the rich in his death, though he had
done no violence, nor was any deceit in his
mouth.

Isaiah 53:9

The entire chapter of Isaiah 53 is prophecy. There are basically two kinds of prophecy, however: 1) when God speaks in the here and now, with reference to the situation at hand; and 2) when he speaks regarding the future. Isaiah 53 is about the future – that is, it *was* the future for Isaiah; it is obviously the past for us. Isaiah lived in 700 BC. He was talking about the event of the Messiah's coming some seven centuries later. God knows the end from the beginning – that is one of the things about God's ways that Isaiah himself was certain of. "I make known the end from the beginning, from ancient times, what is still to come. I say: My purpose will stand and I will do all that I please" (Isaiah 46:10).

Prophecy with regard to the future is sometimes vague enough that nobody can identify the outcome until it happens. Take, for example, the events surrounding the birth of Jesus. The prophets knew that the Messiah would be born in Bethlehem but live in Galilee. No one could figure this out until after Jesus of Nazareth was born in Bethlehem as a consequence of Joseph and Mary having to adhere to the law of Caesar (Luke 2:1ff). But once the events transpired the whole prophetic perspective is clear.

This is the case with Isaiah 53:9. How could the Messiah have a grave with the "wicked" but also with the "rich"? But it is clear to us today!

One of the greatest proofs of the reliability of the Bible is prophecy: how God predicts an event before it happens. There are actually two basic ways by which one comes to affirm the Bible as the infallible word of God: 1) the external proofs; and 2) the internal evidence. The external proofs include things such as archaeology, the Bible's effect on people's lives, or great testimonies of people (how the Bible blessed them, for example). Apologetics is a branch of theology that is designed to prove God's and Jesus' existence and the reliability of the Bible. One should not dismiss apologetics as a way God brings glory to himself.

But the internal evidence of Scripture is more important. John Calvin referred to the "internal testimony of the Holy Spirit" – the Spirit's own witness that the Bible is the word of God. This too may be grasped two ways. First, when the Spirit by an immediate and direct witness testifies to the truth of the Bible. You *know that you know* the Bible is infallibly true. Second, the internal testimony is also to be understood by what Calvin calls the "analogy of faith" (*analogian tes pisteos*, based upon Romans 12:6). This is when one compares Scripture with Scripture and consequently finds the Bible totally reliable. This is an example of the internal, not external, witness, because one believes in the truthfulness and authenticity of the writers themselves throughout the Bible by how they agree with each other. One sees the Bible as the word of God, then, not by what commentators about the Bible say but by what the writers of Scripture say. Sound teaching coheres, whether one is reading from Genesis or Romans, Isaiah or Matthew.

Prophecy may also be understood as having "short-term" predictions and "long-term" ones. An example of a short-term prophecy is when Jesus told the disciples to: "Go to the village ahead of you, and at once you will find a donkey tied there... If anyone says anything to you, tell him that the Lord needs them, and he will send them right away" (Matthew 21:2–3). This was a short-term prophecy in that it was fulfilled moments later: "Those who were sent ahead went and found it just as he had told them" (Luke 19:32). And yet a long-term Old Testament prophecy lay at the bottom of this: "This took place to fulfill what was spoken through the prophet: 'Say to the Daughter of Zion, "See, your king comes to you, gentle and riding on a donkey"'" (Matthew 21:4–5). It was a fulfillment of Zechariah 9:9. The event was fulfilled on Palm Sunday.

Prophecy is a thrilling example of the internal witness of the Spirit, namely, the comparison of Scripture with Scripture. So when it comes to Isaiah 53:9 all we need to do is read the four Gospels – Matthew, Mark, Luke, and John – and see how Isaiah saw certain things in particular seven hundred years in advance.

Although the prophet talked about Jesus' death throughout Isaiah 53, in verse 9 he said that the Messiah would be identified with the wicked and the rich in his death. You may be assured that nobody was thinking of Isaiah 53 when the mobs were shouting: "Crucify him!" Pilate put to them the choice between Barabbas or Jesus. You may recall that it was the governor's custom at the Feast of Passover to release a prisoner chosen by the crowd. Barabbas was a convicted murderer; he deserved to die if anybody did. But the Jews lost their heads and actually asked that Barabbas be released and Jesus crucified. Their request was granted (Matthew 27:26).

Isaiah's reference to the Messiah making his grave with the wicked can in fact be understood in three ways. First, that Jesus was chosen over Barabbas to be crucified. Barabbas had been in prison with the insurrectionists "who had committed murder in the uprising" (Mark 15:7). In the meantime, Pilate's own wife sent a message to her husband: "Don't have anything to do with that innocent man, for

I have suffered a great deal today in a dream because of him" (Matthew 27:19). But in order "to satisfy the crowd", Pilate gave into the crowds and set a murderer free, and commanded Jesus the innocent one to be crucified (Mark 15:15). If anybody – ever – could say "Jesus died for me", it was Barabbas! Jesus literally took Barabbas' place by accepting the punishment Barabbas himself deserved. This then is partly what Isaiah had in mind when he said that the Messiah "made his grave with the wicked" (ESV).

Second, Isaiah's prophecy also pointed to those who were crucified alongside Jesus. It might be forgotten that there were *three* crucifixions on Good Friday. "Two robbers were crucified with him [Jesus], one on his right and one on his left" (Matthew 27:38). Luke records a conversation that took place on Good Friday between the two criminals and Jesus: "One of the criminals who hung there hurled insults at him: 'Aren't you the Christ? Save yourself and us!' But the other criminal rebuked him. 'Don't you fear God,' he said, 'since you are under the same sentence? We are punished justly, for we are getting what our deeds deserve. But this man has done nothing wrong.' Then he said, 'Jesus, remember me when you come into your kingdom.' Jesus answered him, 'I tell you the truth, today you will be with me in paradise'" (Luke 23:39–43). It was one of the most beautiful moments – despite the injustice of Jesus' death – on Good Friday. An instant pardon by Jesus was given to a criminal who would be united with Jesus a few hours later – in paradise (Heaven). It shows that we are saved by the sheer grace of God and not works (Ephesians 2:8–9).

There is yet a third way Isaiah's prophecy could be applied: that Jesus would make his grave with the wicked; he died for sinners. "While we were still sinners, Christ died for us" (Romans 5:8). Indeed, he died for the wicked. Paul actually uses that word, that God "justifies the wicked". Faith counts for righteousness, even when it is exercised by the wicked, says Paul. This means there is hope for you and me! Jesus died for sinners. The ungodly. The wicked. If either the account of Barabbas or the two crucified criminals had not taken place, Jesus dying for you and me would be sufficient to fulfill Isaiah's prophecy.

But what did Isaiah mean by "the rich"? Answer: Joseph of Arimathea, to whom I referred earlier. Three of the four Gospels refer to Joseph. After Jesus was truly dead, "Joseph of Arimathea asked Pilate for the body of Jesus" (John 19:38). "There was a man named Joseph, a member of the Council, a good and upright man, who had not consented to their decision and action. He came from the Judean town of Arimathea... Going to Pilate, he asked for Jesus' body. Then he took it down, wrapped it in linen cloth and placed it in a tomb cut in the rock, one in which no one had yet been laid" (Luke 23:50–53). Matthew calls Joseph a rich man. "As evening approached, there came a rich man from Arimathea, named Joseph, who had himself become a disciple of Jesus. Going to Pilate, he asked for Jesus' body... Joseph took the body, wrapped it in a clean linen cloth, and placed it in his own new tomb that he had cut out of the rock" (Matthew 27:57–60).

Is not this amazing? It is an example of how prophecy is often given with enough vagueness that no one could have thought it up in advance, yet when it is fulfilled it becomes obvious! It is also another example of the "analogy of faith", namely, comparing Scripture with Scripture.

It is an exception to the rule, by the way, that a rich man is saved. Jesus said that "it is easier for a camel to go through the eye of a needle than for a rich man to enter the kingdom of God" (Matthew 19:24). Paul said that not many mighty or noble are called (1 Corinthians 1:26). The Virgin Mary prophesied: "He has filled the hungry with good things but has sent the rich away empty" (Luke 1:53). Like it or not, there is a bias against the rich and for the poor in the New Testament. But there are exceptions. Joseph of Arimathea was one of them. Isaiah saw it seven hundred years in advance. Are you rich – and are saved? Be thankful, because you are the exception to the rule.

Although he was a secret disciple of Jesus – never having confessed him openly, God gave Joseph a chance to do so in the end. He did not dream he was fulfilling prophecy! Perhaps he thought it was too late to go public with his faith now that Jesus had died. All people knew at the time that Jesus had committed no crime, that he didn't deserve to die. But Joseph decided to go public before it was entirely too late – while there would still be a stigma in acknowledging his love for Jesus Christ. Openly – in front of all – he took the dead body of Jesus down from the cross, sending a signal to

Herod, Pilate, the chief priests, and all Jews! When there was nothing in it for him – identifying with a dead man in his burial – he nonetheless testified to his faith in Jesus.

The criminal on the cross who was saved and Joseph of Arimathea had one thing in common: they confessed Jesus when there was still time. The thief on the cross confessed Jesus openly minutes before he died; Joseph of Arimathea did so before Jesus was raised from the dead. Had Joseph not confessed Jesus when he did and then heard of Jesus' resurrection later on, he would have been so ashamed. But he got in "under the wire" – in time to tie his colours to the mast when all thought he was an utter fool for doing so.

Isaiah added: "Though he had done no violence, nor was any deceit in his mouth." Jesus was an innocent man. He never sinned (Hebrews 4:15). Said Peter, "He committed no sin, and no deceit was found in his mouth", a direct reference to Isaiah 53:9 (1 Peter 2:22). Jesus' crime was telling the truth. He never did anything that was remotely deceitful. All he did was to please the Father (John 8:29). "Every day I sat in the temple courts teaching, and you did not arrest me. But this has all taken place that the writings of the prophets might be fulfilled" (Matthew 26:55–56).

All Scripture will be fulfilled. "Heaven and earth will pass away, but my words will never pass away", said Jesus (Matthew 24:35). Jesus too was a prophet. His threefold office was that of prophet, priest, and king. He prophesied of his Second Coming: "No one knows about that day or hour, not even the angels in heaven, nor the Son, but only the Father... So you also must be ready, because the Son of Man will come at an hour when you do not expect him" (Matthew 24:36, 44). In the book of Revelation John saw two categories of people: saved and lost. The lost were those who saw Jesus coming in the clouds and who wailed at the sight of him (Revelation 1:7). But he also saw those who were a multitude "that no one could count, from every nation, tribe, people and language, standing before the throne and in front of the Lamb... and they cried out in a loud voice: 'Salvation belongs to our God, who sits on the throne, and to the Lamb' " (Revelation 7:9–10).

John saw too that the dead, small and great, would stand before God. It was a reference to the Final Judgment. Whereas the thief on the cross who asked to be remembered by Jesus in his kingdom would be saved, the other thief would not be saved. Those whose names were written in the book of life would go to Heaven, all others to Hell (Revelation 20:11–15).

The account of the converted thief on the cross shows that there is such a thing as a "death bed conversion". But there is *only one* such account – that none dare presume; but we do have the one – that all may have hope. The words of Jesus – that the thief would be with him the same day in "paradise" – tells me that a person goes straight – and consciously – to be with Christ the moment he or she dies.

Paul said that if we confess Jesus as Lord and believe in our heart that God raised him from the dead, we will be saved (Romans 10:9). The fact that the thief on the cross asked to be remembered when Jesus came into his kingdom suggests that this thief had implicit faith that Jesus would be raised from the dead. Also, that Joseph of Arimathea would risk his life by confessing Jesus after Jesus *died* tells me that Joseph believed in his heart that Jesus would be raised from the dead; otherwise, why would Joseph do what he did?

We have a Saviour who accepts the cry of anybody when that cry affirms who Jesus is and what he came to do. It is never too late to call on him. But I say that with a caution: do not assume you will be able to do this down the road. "Now is the day of salvation" (2 Corinthians 6:2). "Seek the Lord while he may be found; call on him while he is near" (Isaiah 55:6).

Question: did John see you when he looked and beheld that multitude so great that no person could count it? He saw billions, no doubt. Were you in that vision of John? Years ago I heard a song entitled "Did John see me?" which I found very moving. You will say: "But John had that vision nearly two thousand years ago." Granted. But God knows the end from the beginning and knows your final destiny. And yet you need not be eternally lost. If the Holy Spirit has been moving in your heart with conviction of sin, turn to him now! Confess your sins, repent of them, and put all your eggs into one basket: that Jesus died on the cross for your sins.

CHAPTER TEN

The Legacy of Jesus' Death

Yet it was the Lord's will to crush him and
cause him to suffer, and though the Lord
makes his life a guilt offering, he will see his
offspring and prolong his days, and the will
of the Lord will prosper in his hand.

ISAIAH **53:10**

Legacy means either: 1) leaving a person a gift after one's death; or 2) anything handed down from the past, as from an ancestor or predecessor. The legacy of Jesus embraces both of these meanings. As for leaving a person a gift after one's death, this refers to one's "last will and testament" before they die. The Bible is made up of two "testaments" – Old (thirty-nine books) and New (twenty-seven books). Approximately forty writers over a period of one and a half thousand years have given us our Bible.

The two Testaments are God's will revealed to us. Together, they are his unchanging word. The Bible is God's integrity put on the line. The Old Testament is actually a covenant (*birith* in Hebrew), a contract between two parties still alive. A covenant is usually conditional, based upon acceptance of both parties. The Greek word for "testament" (*diatheke*) is slightly different. It is the legacy of a person based upon their last will but available only after death. It is called a "new covenant". What is new about it is that it is ratified not by one's works but by their acceptance of the conditions of Jesus' last will – namely, that we believe in him.

Isaiah 53 is almost entirely about Jesus' death. It was described by Isaiah as though he wrote it after the event, although it was in fact written seven hundred years before the event. There is more than one way of describing the chapter's theme. You could call it "unashamed of Jesus and the cross". The chapter begins with the question: "Who has believed our message?" Another way of putting this might be: "Who is unashamed of our message?" Most people do not believe the message of the cross. Some are ashamed of it. But are you? Why are we not ashamed? Better still, how *could* we be not ashamed when we consider the legacy of Jesus' death and what it means to us. After all, it is what gives us the gift of Heaven when we die – and which we can never lose. How could anybody be ashamed of him?

The ancient Jews had so looked forward to the coming of the Messiah – their king. They wanted that king to fulfill the glory of his realm. Jesus of Nazareth, who was their king, was in fact born a king. But he did not look like a king to them. He was more of a servant. As a consequence, the Jews rejected the very king they had so looked forward to. The Jews – then and now – have largely rejected the Messiah that was initially offered to them.

The legacy of Jesus began in the will of God. It pleased the Lord God Almighty to bruise him, to crush him. What happened on Good Friday – the historic day that Jesus died on the cross – was by God's pleasure. It pleased the Lord to make him suffer. Perhaps what is pleasing to God has never gripped you very much. It should. I would urge you to make a study of what pleases God. Get on his side. Get into his "skin".

There are two ways of approaching religion, or theology. One is from man's point of view: "What's in it for me?" And that perspective has captivated the world. The other way of looking at it is from God's point of view: "What's in it for God?" Here are some verses in the Bible that ought to grip you and me:

Our God is in heaven; he does whatever pleases him.

(Psalm 115:3)

The Lord does whatever pleases him, in the heavens and on the earth.

(Psalm 135:6)

You, O Lord, have done as you pleased.

(JONAH 1:14)

The Lord was pleased that Solomon had asked for [wisdom].

(1 KINGS 3:10)

For God was pleased to have all his fullness dwell in him.

(COLOSSIANS 1:19)

God was pleased through the foolishness of what was preached to save those who believe.

(1 CORINTHIANS 1:21)

Without faith it is impossible to please God, because anyone who comes to him must believe that he exists and that he rewards those who earnestly seek him.

(HEBREWS 11:6)

I always do what pleases him.

(JOHN 8:29)

The will of God is what pleases God. God was pleased to crush Jesus – his one and only Son – by sending him to the cross. Why would God do this? Because he loves you and me. It is because he loves the world so much. You will say: "Surely he could show his love without having to crush his Son on the cross." I reply: you and I say that for two reasons: 1) we don't understand what sin is; and 2) we are unfamiliar with the ways of the God of the Bible. God said: "My thoughts are not your thoughts, neither are your ways my ways... As the heavens are higher than the earth, so are my ways higher than your ways and my thoughts than your thoughts" (Isaiah 55:8–9).

Until the Holy Spirit comes upon you, you cannot imagine how horrible sin is to God. Sin may not bother us. We may commit sin and feel *nothing*. We may see sin in action and feel *nothing*. Sin is so terrible that no person's good works, turning over a new leaf, trying to be better, New Year's resolutions, or best efforts to get it right will please God. In fact our righteousness is as "filthy rags" to him (Isaiah 64:6). This is not something we can truly grasp until we get to Heaven. In the meantime, we accept God's verdict without quarreling with him. If Isaiah says that it was God's will to crush him, I believe it. I only know that the God of the Bible is not pacified by anything other than his Son becoming an "offering" – which is what Isaiah goes on to say: "the Lord makes his life a guilt offering" ("an offering for sin", in the ESV).

Like it or not, sin cannot be atoned for by our good works or best efforts. If our good works could have saved us, the Mosaic Law would have done it. But it failed – not because there was anything wrong with it but because of us (Romans 8:3). Had our good works been pleasing to God, he would never have sent his Son into the world or willed his death on the cross. *There was no other way.*

The cause of Jesus' death, then, was not the will of the chief priests, the Jews, Herod, Pontius Pilate – or even the devil. The cause was the will of God. "It was the Lord's will to crush him and cause him to suffer." This is the way God accomplished our salvation. Salvation, by the way, means being saved from our *sins*. It is not being saved from poverty, unjust politics, or disease. It pleased the Lord to bruise Jesus because Jesus was made an offering for sin.

Isaiah was explaining how a person becomes a Christian. It is not by education or intelligence. It is not by our good works. It is not because you get into a little bit of trouble and decide to "try God" or "give God a chance" – although God can indeed use difficulty to get our attention. We become a Christian when we see that our sins displease God – and this bothers us. In fact, when the Holy Spirit moves in you may be terrified that your sin goes on and on without your feeling shameful. But once you feel ashamed – and confess your sins – you in that moment dignify Jesus' death on the cross. You affirm his death by being sorry for your sins. This is called repentance – change of mind. Your perspective changes. Pleasing God becomes paramount to you!

It is an old cliché – but here it is: God thought it (in eternity), Jesus Christ bought it (by shedding his blood), and the Holy Spirit wrought it (by convicting us of our sins and pointing us to the cross). It is by grace we are saved, that not of our selves; it is the gift of God – not of works, lest we be boastful (Ephesians 2:8–9).

The curse of Jesus' death is that he was put to grief. There was an ancient assumption: "Anyone who is hung on a tree is under God's curse" (Deuteronomy 21:23). The cross of Jesus is sometimes called a "tree". "He bore our sins in his body on the tree" (1 Peter 2:24). When Jesus hung on the cross – or tree – he was cursed by God. It was when the Lord laid on him our iniquity, as we saw earlier (Isaiah 53:6). God cursed his Son because our sins were laid on him – then he turned his back on Jesus for a moment. It was grief. There was incalculable physical pain for him. If you ask "Why *grief*?" the answer is that that is what sin does – it causes grief. God put his Son to grief – that he might experience the pain, the regret, the shame, the sorrow, and the hopelessness that sin inevitably leads to. Yes, God put his one and only Son to grief on that cross.

> We may not know, we cannot tell, what pains He had
>   to bear;
> But we believe it was for us He hung and suffered
>   there.
>
> CECIL FRANCES ALEXANDER (1818–95)

> O sacred head! Sore wounded, with grief and shame
>   bowed down,
> How scornfully surrounded with thorns, Thine only
>   crown!
> How pale are Thou with anguish, with sore abuse
>   and scorn!

How does that visage languish which once was
bright as morn!

PAUL GERHARDT (1607-76)

The cross of Jesus should be a fairly good hint what God thinks about sin – your sin, my sin. Maybe your sins haven't bothered you all that much. But take note of what God thinks: he put Jesus to grief. And, by the way, may I say this as kindly and lovingly as I know how: grief for sin is what you will feel sooner or later. If you feel it in this life, it will be hard, but that will still not atone for your sin. If you feel it in Hell, that will not atone for your sin. One of the things (I suspect) that will make Hell, Hell is the knowledge of your sins that you loved when you were given a body and life on this planet. But if you grieve for your sins that put Jesus on the cross, then confess them to God, you will be given an instant pardon (1 John 1:9) and a new life to be lived from this day on!

But there is a cure. Jesus was made an "offering for sin". An offering means "sacrifice". In the Old Testament a person brought a sacrifice to the priest – an animal. There are two striking things about the sacrifice brought to the ancient priest. The first is that the priest never examined the person who brought the sacrifice; he examined only the sacrifice. It was the sacrifice that had to be perfect, not the person. Secondly, the person put his hand on the sacrifice. This affirmed the sacrifice as being the cure for one's sins. It was as though one transferred one's sin to the sacrifice –

165

to show the cure.

You need a cure. The cure is outside yourself. It is not enough to say: "I'll try to be better. I will join the church." You must rest your case by trusting that the sacrifice God provided for you – his Son – is adequate. You must believe that you are not examined; the sacrifice is. As long as you are trusting yourself, you have not affirmed the sacrifice. In the words of the hymn:

> Let not conscience make you linger, nor of fitness
>   fondly dream;
> All the fitness He requireth is to feel your need
>   of Him.
> Come ye weary, heavy-laden, bruised and broken by
>   the fall;
> If you tarry till you're better, you will never come
>   at all.
>
> JOSEPH HART (1712–68)

We now look more deeply at the legacy of Jesus' death. What did he will to you as a consequence of his death? He willed for you to have a home in Heaven. "Father," Jesus prayed, "I want those you have given me to be with me where I am, and to see my glory" (John 17:24). This is Jesus' last will and testament – validated only by his death. But he died! You must put your hand on him, as it were – trusting his sacrifice, not yourself. He met the conditions. He was God's perfect lamb. God accepted his sacrifice on the cross.

The first proof of this was that the veil – the curtain in the temple – was rent asunder within a second after Jesus' died (Matthew 27:51). You can rest your case; Jesus' death gives you a legacy – your home in Heaven is secure. It is yours.

But a legacy also refers to what is handed down, what is left after a person has moved on. Isaiah now tells us that Jesus' death was not only no hindrance, but the cause of begetting children. "He will see his offspring." We saw earlier that Jesus had no natural children but a family nonetheless that is more numerous than the sand by the seashore. Isaiah says this again. The crushed Messiah would indeed see his offspring. His earliest disciples included Peter, James, John, Matthew, Thomas, and the rest of the Twelve. God kept all of them except Judas, but Judas' apostasy was also prophesied (John 17:12). If you ask me why God allowed Judas to fall, I have no good answer. But the true disciples of Jesus increased to 120 in the upper room and were filled with the Holy Spirit on the Day of Pentecost. Then three thousand were converted (Acts 2:41). Numbers grew to five thousand after Peter preached following the miracle of a man healed who had never walked (Acts 4:4). Jesus said that the gates of Hell would never prevail against the church (Matthew 16:18). The Christian faith spread all over the Greco-Roman world, into Africa, throughout the Middle East and India, and then to China. It covered all of Europe, and went across the Atlantic to America. It is the dominant religion in Latin America, and the fastest growing in Africa. It is now the largest religion in the world, with 2.3 billion followers of

Christ (one-third of the world's population). That is part of Jesus' legacy.

God would "prolong his days" – a reference to Jesus' resurrection. He died, yes. But he was raised from the dead! You will ask why Isaiah did not simply *say* that the Messiah would be raised from the dead. I answer that prophecy is written in a cryptic fashion *partly* to keep Satan – Jesus' arch-enemy – from figuring out what God was up to. Satan had no idea that God would raise Jesus from the dead. Paul says that God's wisdom is spoken with mystery – a wisdom "hidden". Why? "None of the rulers of this age understood it, for if they had, they would not have crucified the Lord of glory" (1 Corinthians 2:8). Satan would not have engineered the crucifixion of Jesus had he known that Jesus would be resurrected! This explains in part the reason for the cryptic language of prophecy.

God prolonged Jesus' days. Indeed! He is still alive! Jesus now sits at the right hand of God, waiting for the day the Father releases him to return to the earth – which is called the Second Coming of Jesus. Jesus will never – ever – die. Nor will you. Jesus' resurrection guarantees that all will be raised from the dead – and live forever.

The same will of God that put Jesus to grief will also guarantee his prosperity. "The will of the Lord will prosper in his hand." This means that Jesus cannot be ultimately defeated. If God be for us, who can be against us (Romans 8:31). Those who rely on Jesus will never be ashamed (Romans 10:11). God will never leave us (Hebrews 13:5).

Jesus will never leave us (Matthew 28:20). All our needs will be supplied (Philippians 4:19). "For no matter how many promises God has made, they are 'Yes' in Christ" (2 Corinthians 1:20). The atonement of Jesus Christ has given us everything we need. God's will to crush him has been vindicated.

CHAPTER ELEVEN

Justification by Faith

After the suffering of his soul, he will see the
light of life and be satisfied; by his knowledge
my righteous servant will justify many, and
he will bear their iniquities.

ISAIAH 53:11

The prophet now focuses on a very important teaching, one that has been implicit throughout Isaiah 53 – justification by faith. The name Martin Luther (1483–1546) is largely associated with this teaching. Although it was a rediscovery of truth as far as the Bible is concerned, it was new to Luther. He saw that faith "alone" satisfied the justice of God. It turned his world, and, eventually, the western world, upside down. Europe and western civilization was never to be the same again.

The teaching of justification by faith alone is possibly the hardest doctrine of all for the church to maintain. Here is why: it seems too good to be true. The fear of antinomianism (lawlessness), that if you have faith it does not matter how you live, threatened this teaching. And yet Dr Martyn Lloyd-Jones taught that if our Gospel is not *accused* of being antinomian, chances are people haven't understood it yet or we haven't really preached it! Whereas Luther's teaching turned Europe and England upside down in the sixteenth century, it passed behind a cloud in the seventeenth century. The reason: the English Puritans came up with a parallel notion – namely, that we need to *know* whether or not we *have* justifying faith. The issue of "assurance" emerged. It is one thing to be justified by faith, they said, but do you have *assurance* that your faith is truly the faith that justifies? In other words, whereas it was widely assumed that faith alone justifies, the Puritans taught that you needed to be sure you truly had "justifying" faith and not a counterfeit belief. The way to know you had this faith, they generally taught, was by your sanctification. Good works. So if sanctification was there – or sufficient good works – you may conclude that you have justifying faith. The problem was that conscientious Christians everywhere said: "I am not sure my sanctification is sufficient to warrant that I have justifying faith." The joy of this teaching therefore faded and endless introspection set in. It was so sad. For those who want to go into this more deeply, please take a look at my *Calvin and English Calvinism to 1648*, first published by Oxford University Press and now available from Paternoster Press. Also, my little book *He Saves* (Hodder & Stoughton) goes into more detail than space will allow in this chapter.

I must say, too, that the doctrine of justification by faith again largely remains behind a cloud in the twenty-first century. Other teachings – with emphases on politics, prosperity, or orthodoxy (evangelicalism versus liberalism) – have competed with it. In my travels all over the world I have been increasingly alarmed at how vague the teaching on justification by faith is in churches, and how few people grasp it. It needs to be revived and we can only pray that when God visits the church in power again there will be a sufficient number of people to uphold it, so that the church can turn the world upside down one more time before the Second Coming.

We will now explore this teaching somewhat more deeply than previously in this book. I would like to introduce this teaching as if you the reader had never heard of it before. But before Isaiah comes to his phrase "my righteous servant will justify many", he introduces it with a reference to the "soul" of the Messiah.

"After the suffering of his soul, he will see the light of life and be satisfied." The reference to his *soul* refers to Christ's mental anguish, his emotional turmoil, and the challenge to his inner strength. We have noted the physical sufferings of Jesus in this book. But Isaiah 53:11 brings up the sufferings of Jesus' soul. This aspect of his suffering was not limited to the ordeal of the cross. It was what Jesus lived with the whole of his life. When the writer of the epistle to the Hebrews states that Jesus was tempted at all points like you and me but without sin (Hebrews 4:15), it was a reference to every type of temptation: sex, pride, self-pity, and unbelief.

Take sexual temptation, for example. You may want to say that Jesus resisting sexual temptation was easy for him since he was the God-man. Wrong. It was not easy. He was fully a man. Whereas Jesus was God as though he were not man, he was man as though he were not God. I can safely predict that when we get to Heaven we will be given a glimpse of how hard it was for him. The pain of sexual temptation is heightened because it is physical, natural, and also relates to one's self-esteem and loneliness. Jesus achieved complete victory over sexual temptation. But what was it all for? I reply: that he could be the perfect sacrifice on the cross. Had Jesus sinned even once – in thought, word, or deed – he could not have atoned for our sins. It was required in the Mosaic Law that an animal must be perfect and without any defects (Exodus 12:5). The Lamb of God was precisely that – "without blemish or defect" (1 Peter 1:19). Peter could say therefore that Jesus "committed no sin, and no deceit was found in his mouth" (1 Peter 2:22). Therefore when Jesus was hanging on the cross – despite the physical pain and anguish of his soul – he was "satisfied". He knew he had passed the test. He knew he had pleased the Father. So when he uttered those words, "It is finished", just before he breathed his last breath (John 19:30), it was a conscious triumph. It meant Mission Accomplished! What satisfaction it gave him. Yes, he saw the travail of his soul and was "satisfied".

Jesus' pride and self-esteem was challenged throughout his days on this earth. Take the way his brothers (that is, his half-brothers) treated him, for example. They challenged him to go to Jerusalem to display his miraculous powers, for "no one who wants to become a public figure acts in secret". It was a poisonous, vicious, and false accusation, which implied that Jesus aspired to be a famous person. Nothing could be further from the truth. He made himself "nothing", making himself of "no reputation" (Philippians 2:5–7, AV). Had Jesus retorted – or pointed the finger at his brothers in defence – it would have been a sin. It would have disqualified him from being our Saviour. But he resisted the temptation all the way to the cross – and had with it the inner satisfaction that he finished the work the Father gave him to do (John 4:34).

He knew rejection not only from sibling rivalry but from all the Jews and Pharisees generally. Rolfe Barnard (1903–69) used to say that Jesus fell back on the doctrine of election for his comfort when being rejected right, left and centre by the Jews. Jesus could say, "All that the Father gives me *will* come to me" (John 6:37). He knew that those *not* given to him by the Father would *not* be coming, but only those that had been chosen. He therefore never took rejection personally, knowing the reason the Pharisees did not believe in him. "How can you believe [in me] if you accept praise from one another, yet make no effort to obtain the praise that comes from the only God?" (John 5:44). Jesus knew that it was because their priority was seeking praise from one another – not seeking God's glory – that they were unable to believe.

Consider too his role as a leader. Jesus had three years of non-stop sorting out the Twelve – their picayune complaints, their inability to see what he was teaching, their rivalry among themselves, their self-righteousness, and their rejection of him in the end (Matthew 26:56). In his loneliness he appealed to his inner circle (Peter, James, and John) in the Garden of Gethsemane, hoping to have their support in his darkest hour – but they slept through the whole thing (Matthew 26:36–45). What inner strength Jesus had when he could see right through every single one of them and not show it! He knew that Simon Peter – his most illustrious follower – would deny him in a few hours, but never took it personally. "I have prayed for you," he could say to Peter in the same moment (Luke 22:32–34). Had he given in to self-pity for a moment it would have been a sin. But he never did. His reward: satisfaction when hanging on the cross. And satisfaction long after that!

Jesus lived by a perfect faith. Everything he did was to please the Father (John 8:29). Isaiah said that by the Messiah's *"knowledge* my righteous servant will justify many"*. You will say: I thought it was my faith! True. But behind our faith is his faith. Isaiah calls it "knowledge". Why? It was because *faith is* knowledge. John Calvin (1509–64) defined faith as "sure knowledge". Jesus' faith was not an opaque, doubting, vague, or speculative guessing of what to do next. He *knew* what his calling was, he *knew* what his mission was, he *knew* the Father's will, he *knew* he had pleased the Father, he *knew* the details of the Mosaic Law, he *knew* he had fulfilled it, and he *knew* who he was. Had he doubted at any time during his thirty-three years, such unbelief would have been a sin. But he never doubted. He went to the cross having fully believed he had pleased the Father perfectly. This is why those words "It is finished" were triumphant. You will recall from a previous chapter that the Greek *tetelestai* was a colloquial expression in the ancient market place that meant "paid in full". The travail and anguish of his soul was worth it all! He had dreaded the cross. But in the physical torture of it all he had inner peace that he pleased the Father.

Did Jesus have this satisfaction only when he uttered the words "It is finished"? He had it before then. He received the immediate and direct witness from the Father periodically. At his baptism the voice from Heaven said "This is my Son, whom I love; with him I am well pleased" (Matthew 17:5). As for John the Baptist, he doubted (Luke 7:20). But Jesus never doubted. When he was transfigured before his inner circle that voice came from Heaven: "This is my Son, whom I love; with him I am well pleased" (Matthew 3:17). Without faith it is impossible to please God (Hebrews 11:6), but Jesus pleased God by his perfect faith, sinless life, and total obedience all the way to death on the cross. His vindication was not external. That would have meant affirmation by the Pharisees, Sadducees, Herod, and Pilate. His vindication was internal. It is what Paul calls "vindication by the Spirit"

(1 Timothy 3:16). He did not need the approval of people to bolster his faith.

Therefore Jesus would justify many by his knowledge. This meant that his perfect faith lay behind our justification. But you might still say: "I thought it was our faith that justified us." Granted. But his faith came first! This is why Paul said that the righteousness of God is revealed "from faith to faith" (Romans 1:17, AV). This means Jesus' faith and our faith. All that Jesus did for us would be of no value unless we too believed. Our faith ratifies his faith. To ratify means "to put into effect". What Jesus did by believing perfectly for us, obeying perfectly for us, and dying as the spotless Lamb for us had to be ratified by our reliance on his life and death or we would not be saved. We are saved by his life and his death (Romans 5:10). His death would have been of no value had he not lived and believed perfectly. His life would have been of no value had he not taken the punishment for our sins on the cross.

Jesus is our justifier. But did not Luther teach we are justified by faith? Yes. Dr Martyn Lloyd-Jones also pointed out: "We are justified by Christ." John Calvin taught there are three "causes" for our justification: 1) the meritorious cause – what Jesus did; 2) the instrumental cause – our faith; and 3) the efficient cause – the Holy Spirit. We are justified when the Holy Spirit moves on us and *enables* us to believe. Faith is but the instrument that achieves our being made righteous. The meritorious cause is Jesus Christ – he is the one who will justify many.

Who are the "many"? As we will see below, "many" and "all" can sometimes be used interchangeably. But if Jesus justified *all*, why are not all saved? Answer: because they do not believe. Jesus died for all, he believed for all. But the righteousness of God is revealed "from faith to faith". Our faith must kick in (to use a vernacular expression) or there will be no justification. None. This is why we believe in justification by faith; my faith must rest in Christ or his righteousness will not be put to my credit. Faith is the sure knowledge of God's graciousness to us in the cross. We look to the death of Christ for our salvation. The moment we do this we are justified.

Paul referred to Abraham as proof that this was not new teaching. As Abraham believed the promise, and it counted for righteousness (Genesis 15:6), Paul taught that when we believe the Gospel our faith counts for righteousness (Romans 4:5). The moment we truly believe, we are given an instant pardon! In that moment the righteousness of Christ is imputed to us, put to our credit *as though we are as righteous as Christ*. But do not works play a part? No. Paul immediately pointed out that Abraham's justification came *before* he was circumcised (Romans 4:9–12). This was very important to Paul. Circumcision would have been a "work" – indeed, it was commanded work. But Abraham's justification was already an unchangeable fact! This is why Paul could say we are saved by grace through faith and not works (Ephesians 2:8–9).

But you will ask: where do works come in? Paul replies:

"We are God's workmanship, created in Christ Jesus to do good works" (Ephesians 2:10). The same God who chose us and sent the Spirit to give us life isn't finished; we are his workmanship, and good works will inevitably *follow* faith. If they must precede faith – or serve as a condition of justifying faith – every honest, conscientious, and transparent person would have *some* doubt whether there are sufficiently good works to warrant our claiming to be justified by faith. God puts us on our honour that we will live lives of gratitude to him. Our sanctification is a grateful response to the Gospel, not a condition of salvation. Otherwise, who can ever know for sure that he or she is saved?

But when we are justified, it *extends* our Lord's satisfaction. This is because he rose from the dead, ascended to Heaven and sits at the right hand of God. When someone on earth relies on his death it gives our Lord further satisfaction. He therefore saw the anguish of his soul and was satisfied by his life and triumph on the cross; he continues to be "satisfied". Yes, every time a person transfers their trust from good works to Jesus' death it means he is again "satisfied"! You and I bring great satisfaction to our Lord by our reliance upon his faith.

> This is my Father's world, O let me ne'er forget
> That though the wrong seems oft so strong,
> God is the Ruler yet.
> This is my Father's world,
> The battle is not done;

Jesus who died shall be satisfied,
And earth and heav'n be one.

MALTBIE D. BABCOCK (1858–1901)

This is why Paul said we have believed in Jesus Christ in order that we might be justified by the "faith of Christ" (Galatians 2:16, AV). Christ's faith and our faith must go together – or there will be no justification.

Isaiah adds: "he will bear their iniquities". This may well be an intentional repetition or summary of what he has been saying throughout Isaiah 53, certainly reiterating the promise that the Lord laid on him the "iniquity of us all", as in verse 6. But I think Isaiah means more than that. Jesus is now at the right hand of God and continues to uphold our case before the Father by his continual intercession. He died once, for all. But at the Father's right hand our Lord lives ever to beckon for the attention of the Father to look at him, to keep the Father's "gaze away from our sins", as Calvin put it. This is why Paul could say he is not only justified by the faith of Christ, but *"lives* by the faith of the Son of God" (Galatians 2:20, AV).

It is not great faith that is required of you and me. Christ had that. It is relying on a great Saviour that is required of us. You simply rely on what Jesus did, not what you have done – and rest your case with him!

I need no other argument, I need no other plea;
It is enough that Jesus died, and that He died for
me.

LIDIE H. EDMUNDS (1851–1920)

CHAPTER TWELVE

The Vindication of Jesus Christ

Therefore I will give him a portion among
the great, and he will divide the spoils with
the strong, because he poured out his life
unto death, and was numbered with the
transgressors. For he bore the sin of many,
and made intercession for the transgressors.

ISAIAH 53:12

In this final verse of Isaiah 53 we are immediately taken from Jesus' death on the cross to his position at the right hand of God. "Therefore I will give him a portion among the great." This statement shows Jesus alive and well after his death. But Isaiah says more: he "made intercession for the transgressors" – which points to the Messiah's role as our Great High Priest at the Father's right hand. The "I" is a reference to God speaking. "I will give him a portion among the great" is another affirmation of the Son from God the Father.

Isaiah 53:12 refers to Jesus' vindication. This verse assumes he is not only alive but also receiving his inheritance. Now that the Messiah has been smitten, crushed, and cut off, then, Isaiah refers to Jesus' reward. It was what the writer of Hebrews calls "the joy set before him", that is, what Jesus was looking forward to. Though our Lord Jesus despised the shame, he knew what would follow this – namely, his inheritance, or reward. It was another way of showing that he saw the travail of his soul and was "satisfied".

Vindication means to be absolved from blame after being falsely accused. It means having your name cleared. The Jews accused Jesus of blasphemy for claiming he was God. The truth: Jesus was – and is – God. Indeed. The writer of Hebrews talks about the "name" Jesus inherited (Hebrews 1:4). That name is Yahweh. "Therefore God exalted him to the highest place and gave him the *name that is above every name*, that at the name of Jesus every knee should bow, in heaven and on earth and under the earth, and every tongue confess that Jesus Christ is Lord, to the glory of God the Father" (Philippians 2:9–11). When we confess that Jesus Christ is "Lord", we are affirming him to have that name which is above every name, namely "Yahweh". That is as high as it gets.

So Isaiah 53 begins with the root out of dry ground – so inconspicuous and lacklustre that the prophet knew the Messiah would be rejected. But Isaiah ends triumphantly:

with Jesus being openly vindicated and receiving his reward before the entire population – of every human being who ever lived!

The translation should read: "I will give him a portion among the *many*" (as in the ESV). How many? All! *"Every* knee shall bow and *every* tongue shall confess." That means everybody! We saw above that "many" and "all" are sometimes used interchangeably. This is an example of this. No human being who ever lived – no demonic power – will be exempt from proclaiming who Jesus is.

The scholar H. C. Leupold reckoned that no passage in the Old Testament presents more problems than this verse. The Jews did not know how to interpret this baffling verse. But Isaiah is referring to their Messiah who died on a cross and then took on the role of high priest! "You are a priest for ever, in the order of Melchizedek" (Psalm 110:4). We saw this earlier, but now Isaiah closes this glorious chapter of his by referring to Jesus' kingly and priestly position at the Father's right hand. That is what he means by making "intercession for the transgressors".

I would like to share a very personal story. When I was doing my theological research at Oxford, after my third year I developed a hypothesis regarding the teaching of John Calvin. I had been reading the Puritans day and night, and would dip into Calvin in between. I noticed a difference between Calvin and these men. I became convinced – but without any explicit evidence – that John Calvin must have believed that Jesus died for everybody but interceded only for God's elect. By dying for everybody, I mean literally all people, not just some. This went against traditional opinion. And yet I was equally convinced that Calvin also believed that Jesus did not intercede for everybody at God's right hand – but only some (God's chosen). But I needed positive proof if I was going to make a scholarly case at Oxford. One Friday night – late – in Regent's Park College library, I came across Calvin's commentary on Isaiah 53:12, the same verse I am now expounding. There it was! Calvin wrote (you can read this both in his commentary and in his sermon on Isaiah 53:12, showing that he said it both times) that the "many" means "all" when Isaiah said that the Messiah bore the sin of "many". But that the intercession was not for the world (Calvin referred to John 17:9 where Jesus said he did not pray for the world) but for the elect. Jesus died for all but interceded for the elect only. That is what Isaiah 53:12 is saying. That the Messiah would make "intercession for the transgressors" refers to his priestly work at God's right hand.

Calvin applied Isaiah 53:12 to the ancient Day of Atonement (see Leviticus 16). Calvin likened Christ bearing the sin of many to the high priest making a sacrifice of blood on the open altar. Calvin then applied the reference to making intercession for transgressors to the high priest going behind the veil into the Most Holy Place. To summarize: the animal was slain openly on the altar – which prefigured Jesus' death on the cross. But the atonement did not "take effect" on the Day of Atonement until the high priest took the blood behind the curtain. So Jesus died for everybody (John 3:16; 2 Corinthians 5:14–15; Hebrews 2:9). But his intercession was carried out for those who believed: namely, those God had chosen.

Isaiah 53:12 is "post-battle language", as one commentator put it. "Therefore" refers to his anguish of soul, his painful suffering – everything that Jesus went through during his life and death. But now that suffering is over. "Therefore I will give him a portion among the many." He was vindicated! The scene is one of the distribution of the spoils after a decisive victory has been won. The suffering servant has been rewarded and receives his well-deserved share – the lion's share!

"He will divide the spoils with the strong." This means that we share in Christ's inheritance. We are co-heirs with Jesus, according to Paul, because we have been adopted into the family. We are God's children. "Now if we are children, then we are heirs – heirs of God and co-heirs with Christ, if indeed we share in his sufferings in order that we may also share in his glory" (Romans 8:15). His glory includes his open vindication before the world and victory over Satan. Every knee bowing and every tongue confessing "on earth and under the earth" (Philippians 2:10) must refer to Satan and all demonic forces. One translation has it: "he will receive the mighty as spoil" (Apologetics Bible).

Satan deceived the human race. He blinds the minds of every person lest they see the glory of Christ (2 Corinthians 4:4). The division of the spoil by the Lord Jesus Christ partly means his rescuing souls from Satan's grasp. He carries out the Father's will as intercessor. Those who come to God by him are those for whom Jesus intercedes. If you ask "How do I know Jesus intercedes for me since he did not intercede for everybody?" then I answer: "He prays for all those who trust his blood." His blood was shed for all men and women. All you need to do is to claim an interest in that blood. It is your right as much as it is that of any person who ever lived – regardless of their class, colour, education, or intelligence. Not only that; Jesus intercedes for all who come to God by him (Hebrews 7:25). Don't ask "Is Jesus interceding for me?" but ask: "Am I coming to God by him?" Those who trust his blood (not their works) and come to the Father through Jesus Christ (for there is no other way – John 14:6) are those who will inherit with Jesus.

The powers of darkness will be totally defeated one day. But evil prevails as I write these lines. You should know what actually went on behind the scenes as a consequence of Jesus' death. "When you ascended on high, you led captives in your train", prophesied David (Psalm 68:18). The blood Jesus shed "disarmed the powers and authorities". Jesus made "a public spectacle of them, triumphing over them by the cross" (Colossians 2:15). This is why Satan hates the blood of Jesus. That which he thought gave him his victory – crucifying Jesus – is precisely what gave him his defeat. By Jesus' death he took authority over him "who holds the power of death – that is, the devil – and free[d] those who all their lives were held in slavery by their fear of death" (Hebrews

2:14–15). "I am the Living One," he said to John on the Isle of Patmos, "I was dead, and behold I am alive for ever and ever! And I hold the keys of death and Hades" (Revelation 1:18). Those who interpreted Holy Scripture in the earliest church only had the Old Testament to go by. Isaiah 53:12 gave them immense comfort! So too Psalm 16:10: "You will not abandon me to the grave, nor will you let your Holy One see decay" – a reference to Jesus' resurrection (Acts 2:27). Jesus was declared to be the Son of God by his resurrection from the dead (Romans 1:4). Then he ascended to the right hand of God – to which Isaiah 53:12 refers.

So where is Jesus now? He is at the Father's right hand – reigning as King and interceding as our Great High Priest.

Hebrews 2:8 states that God "left nothing that is not subject to him. Yet at present we do not see everything subject to him." True. Jesus has ascended to the right hand of God. He reigns. He intercedes for us. But the world is still not subject to him. Evil abounds. Poverty prevails. Injustice thrives. Corrupt politicians manage to stay in office. Unfair judges get away with wicked and unjust decisions. Earthquakes, famine and hurricanes destroy. Where is God? Why does he let these things happen? "We do not see everything subject to him." Quite. But, says Isaiah, owing to the anguish of Jesus' soul and torture of his body, because he bore the sin of many, he will ascend to God's right hand. This is prerequisite to his open vindication.

But Jesus' position at God's right hand is a temporary one. He will not be there forever and ever. He is waiting for a day. It will be the Day of Days. He himself admitted that he did not know the day or the hour, that only the Father knows (Matthew 24:36). But there is coming a day when God will instruct an angel to get a trumpet ready. The black slaves in the Deep South of America reckoned it would be blown by Gabriel. Some think it will be silver. I don't know its colour or who will blow it. But in a moment that no one suspects, there will be the voice of an archangel that will be heard around the world and the sound of a trumpet that will awaken the dead. Jesus will vacate his place at God's right hand and show himself openly to the world. Every eye shall see him. Those who pierced him will see him. All peoples of the earth will wail and mourn for him. They will fall on their knees. They will scream. They will plead. They will pray like they have never prayed. For Jesus will show himself alive and well to all people – living and dead – on planet earth. This is what Isaiah saw seven hundred years before Christ. You and I will share in all this. We will not be among those crying and pleading. It will be our vindication too.

All this would happen, said Isaiah, because the Suffering Servant "poured out his life unto death". On that Good Friday, the Jews said: "He got what was coming to him." Those loved ones at the cross – such as his mother and Mary Magdalene – could not take it in. The demons of Hell rejoiced. But on Easter morning Jesus was resurrected. He remained on earth for forty days, then ascended to Heaven. He took his place at God's right hand. That is where he is as you read these lines. Even now his vindication is by the

Spirit (1 Timothy 3:16) since only believers by the work of the Holy Spirit believe what you are now reading. But there is coming a day when his vindication will be open – nothing hidden – and for all to see.

He was "numbered with the transgressors". This means two things: 1) his crucifixion was between two criminals – which Isaiah no doubt was partly referring to; and 2) Jesus identified with all sinners. He was numbered with them – pleading "guilty" to their sins. Whether it was murder, stealing, child abuse, illicit sex, rape, cruelty, lying, or being a dictator who killed millions of innocent people, Jesus bore all these sins. God charged Jesus with these sins. He bore these sins. He paid for them by his blood.

"Therefore," says Isaiah, "I will give him a portion with the many." It will be an open, visible vindication. Every human being – small and great, saint and wicked, famous and unknown, of any colour, race and creed – will get down on their knees and acknowledge that Jesus Christ is LORD – *Yahweh* – to the glory of God the Father. All because of the travail of his soul.

God loves to vindicate. It is what he does best. I can hardly wait. What about you? I can tell you this much: you will see it. Whether you are saved or lost, you will witness Jesus' vindication. It will be the day God clears his name. It will be the day God wipes away our tears. There will be no more death, crying, or pain. Those days will be over – forever and ever.

You have an opportunity to know what your state will

be on that Day. You can know now. In this book I have given you a prayer to pray. It is at the end of Chapter Three. Don't put it off.

The Suffering Servant – the Lord Jesus Christ – wants to be your Saviour, Lord, and friend. He will come into your heart right now. Just invite him. You can then begin to look forward to Jesus' vindication. And yours too, because all of us who have sided with Jesus Christ – and been laughed at in the meantime – will be openly vindicated. Jesus will share his inheritance with us. God will clear your name on that Day. For this reason: Jesus died and you relied on his blood.

May God Almighty – Father, Son, and Holy Spirit – bless you in this moment. Now and forever. Amen.